The Four Types of Narcissism

Understanding the Narcissistic Personality Disorder
and Introducing Revolutionary Ways for
Extraordinary Emotional Abuse Recovery

GEOFFREY LOREN

© Copyright 2019 - All rights reserved.

The content contained within this book may not be reproduced, duplicated or transmitted without direct written permission from the author or the publisher.

Under no circumstances will any blame or legal responsibility be held against the publisher, or author, for any damages, reparation, or monetary loss due to the information contained within this book, either directly or indirectly.

Legal Notice:

This book is copyright protected. It is only for personal use. You cannot amend, distribute, sell, use, quote or paraphrase any part, or the content within this book, without the consent of the author or publisher.

Disclaimer Notice:

Please note the information contained within this document is for educational and entertainment purposes only. All effort has been executed to present accurate, up to date, reliable, complete information. No warranties of any kind are declared or implied. Readers acknowledge that the author is not engaging in the rendering of legal, financial, medical or professional advice. The content within this book has been derived from various sources. Please consult a licensed professional before attempting any techniques outlined in this book.

By reading this document, the reader agrees that under no circumstances is the author responsible for any losses, direct or indirect, that are incurred as a result of the use of information contained within this document, including, but not limited to, errors, omissions, or inaccuracies.

Table of Contents

Introduction 1

Chapter 1: Where Does NPD Come From? 9

What is Narcissism? 9

    What is Narcissistic Personality Disorder (NPD)? 10

    Causes of NPD 11

    A Narcissist's Childhood: Neglectful or Overindulgent Parents 12

    Parenting Styles that Promote Narcissism 15

Common Traits of NPD 20

    They are Constantly Trying to Make Others Look Bad 20

    They Get Angry When Things Don't Go Their Way 21

    They Have an Insincere Charm 21

    They Continually Tell Lies and Exaggerate 22

    They Inflict Emotional Suffering 22

    False Projection 23

    They Resort to Aggression and Denial When Criticized on their Flaws 24

    They have no Respect for Boundaries or Rules 25

Is Narcissism a Survival Technique? 26

Chapter 2: What Really Goes Through a Narcissists Mind? 30

Living in Their Little World 30

Adding Gas to the Fire 33

    How Do They Get Their Fuel? 34

    How do They Leave Their Victims? 35

    How do Narcissists Exhibit Dependency? 36

    How Do They Gain and Maintain Control? 36

    Getting a New Source 37

    Why do Narcissists often End up with Past Victims? 39

    Is the Source Limited to Providing Emotional Needs? 39

    Does Negativity Count Toward the Narcissistic Supply? 40

    Narcissists and Past Sources 41

Some of the Things that Scares the Narcissist 42

    Commitment to a Relationship 42

    Self-Reflection 42

    Receiving Insults 42

    Shame 43

    Lack of Attention 43

    Having Their Lies Exposed 44

    Showing Gratitude 44

Chapter 3: 5 Incredibly Destructive Tactics Narcissists Will Use to Bring You Down 45

False Self, True Self 45

Idealization, Devaluation, Discard 48

Gaslighting 51

Getting the Victim on the Defensive 52

Repeating the Lies 52

Misdirection and Escalation..................................... 52

Get You to Back Down 53

Make You Codependent.. 53

A Sense of Remorse 54

Assume the Role of a Puppeteer.............................. 55

Triangulation.. 55

Smear Campaigns 57

Your Family... 58

Your Workplace 58

Court Proceedings 59

Your Friends.. 59

Chapter 4: The Grandiose Narcissist 61

Key Traits and Behaviors 63

They Have Low Neuroticism.................................... 63

They Exhibit High Extroversion 64

They Have a Low Agreeableness 64

They Are Manipulative.. 65

Exaggerated Sense of Self-Importance...................... 65

They Try to Dominate 66

They Appear to be Self-Sufficient 66

Chapter 5: The Malignant Narcissist 68

Key Traits and Behaviors.. 70

They Are Sadistic Individuals 70

They are Manipulative 71

Their Feeling of Empathy is Nonexistent 72

An Unhealthy Sense of Superiority.......................... 73

They are Paranoid 74

They Exhibit Antisocial Behaviors........................... 75

They are Envious of Others...................................... 75

They are Extremely Charming Individuals 76

They Don't Like Criticism 76

They Engage in Psychological Projection................. 77

They Refuse to Admit to any Wrongdoing.............. 77

They are Egocentric.. 78

They Need People to Pay Attention to Them.......... 79

Chapter 6: The Covert Narcissist................................. 80

Key Traits and Behaviors... 82

They are Extremely Sensitive Individuals................. 82

They are Passive Aggressive 83

Smugness 87

They Don't Show Empathy 89

An Unusual Feeling of Self-Importance 90

They form Detached Relationships 90

They are Self-Absorbed 92

Chapter 7: The Communal Narcissist 94

Explicit and Implicit Views in Communal
Narcissism 94

The Communal Narcissism Inventory 96

Key Traits and Behaviors 98

They Get Their Supply from Engaging in
Communal Work 98

They are Constantly Talking about how
Helpful They are to Others 99

They Consider Themselves as Givers and
Not Takers 100

Their Private Life Differs from their Public 100

Chapter 8: Understanding What Obstacles You Need to Overcome 101

Lack of Boundaries 101

Psychological Trap 103

Starvation for Love 104

Low Shame Tolerance and Low Self Esteem 106

Fear and Guilt 107

Lacking a Sense of Shame 110

Chapter 9: Create an Indestructible Support Structure and Restore Your Self-Esteem 112

Find Allies and Friends 112
    How the Narcissist gets your friends 113
    Getting Past Isolation 114

Find Support Groups and Talk to People Who Are Going Through the Same Thing 116
    Why should you join a support group? 117
    How do you choose the right support group? 118
    Are there signs that can act as red flags when selecting a support group? 119
    Choosing an online support group over one that requires a physical presence 119
    Getting Information on Helpful Support Groups 121

Restore Self-Esteem 122

Chapter 10: Breaking Out of an Unbreakable Trap .. 127

Emotional Investment Mismatch and Trap 128
    Understanding the Emotional Investment Trap 131

Humor Trap 132

Conversation Trap 133

Refuse to Take the Bait 134
    Dodging the Emotional Investment Trap 135
    Shutting Down the Humor Trap 136

Escaping the Conversation Trap 137

Chapter 11: Creating Ironclad Boundaries That Will Last 138

Drawing the Line... 139

Defining Your Boundaries 141

Make Use of an If/When List 143

Stop Stroking the Narcissists' Ego............ 144

Using the Gray Rock Method to Put up a Boundary.. 145

Limit the Amount of Information you Feed the Narcissist..................................... 147

Stick to it! 147

Try to Understand the Narcissist 149

Leave if You Have To 149

Conclusion 153

References... 159

Introduction

One of the problems some people experience in a relationship is abuse. This abuse can come from parents, a spouse, or a caretaker. A form of abuse that leaves lasting damage on the victims is the narcissistic abuse.

Like other forms of abuse, this can come from those you hold dear. The problem with narcissistic abuse is the difficulty in identifying those who are responsible for it. These are the people you know as the narcissists.

Narcissists appear like everyone else on the outside–charming, friendly, successful, and attractive. Depending on the origin of abuse, parents or spouse, the first step in escaping this abuse is understanding the narcissist.

To fully understand the narcissist, you must look beyond the superficial mask of the narcissist.

- Why are they like this?
- Does their childhood affect their personality?
- What are they hiding beneath their mask?
- Why do they often like to attract attention?
- Can I be under the manipulation of a narcissist without my knowing?

- Am I at fault for the abuse?
- Why doesn't the narcissist show me any form of love, affection, or emotion?
- Am I the only victim of their abuse?
- Is there a possibility of changing their personality?

These are some of the questions that pop up when dealing with a narcissist. The lack of answers to this question is one of the problems that make it difficult for you to deal with the narcissist.

Another problem is learning to get over the narcissist in your life. These individuals are incredibly manipulative and great at conditioning using various traps. These traps make it challenging to live a healthy life after going no contact on the narcissist. Other traps are also in place to make you joyous anytime the narcissist comes calling despite the level of abuse you go through.

With battered self-esteem, financial instability, and starvation of love–some of the effects of the abuse, you are left picking up the pieces of your life. This is where you must begin your healing process after your relationship with the narcissist. But how do you do this?

This is the final problem you are going to encounter when dealing with the narcissist—healing yourself of the damage from the relationship. This is the hardest part of dealing with a narcissist and is also one of the reasons most victims end up jumping into another narcissistic relationship in the future.

In this book, you will find the answers to all the questions on your mind. Herein, you will find information to help you get a grasp on the concept of narcissism. These include learning about narcissistic personality disorder, the four major types of narcissists, and how the narcissists objectify people to get their supply.

In the narcissistic relationship, you keep doing the most without realizing that it is due to the effect of manipulation from the narcissist. They will get you to give in to all their demands, provide their needs, and never question their authority. If you falter in any of these areas, they will resort to ridicule, neglect, and abuse as a means of exerting punishment and putting you down.

To protect yourself from these actions, I am going to help you learn and understand how to put up effective boundaries in addition to creating support structures. Other things I will introduce are the obstacles that you must overcome and traps you must break free of when engaging in your recovery to end the abuse.

The narcissistic personality disorder is often noticeable in those that you love and cherish. This is a fact, and I am saying this from experience. This experience is from living with a narcissist while growing up, from my early childhood to my early adult life.

The narcissist in my life happened to be my father. Despite the unconditional love I have for him, the truth remains that my father was an extreme grandiose narcissist–the first narcissist I will ever know in life.

In getting to understand and relate better with my father, I have dedicated years of my life to look into the narcissistic personality disorder. These years of my life coincide with a part of my early adult life. That is the time of my life during which I had to understand my father better and also undergo recovery from the narcissistic abuse he put me through.

Understanding what most victims of narcissistic abuse go through, I am incredibly passionate about offering as much help as I can. This is to ensure that you can manage the narcissist in your life and still live a better life afterward.

In life, perspective is usually a determinant in success and failure. Without a change in your perspective, you may never truly overcome narcissistic abuse. That is what you get after completing this book–a change in your outlook on life with a narcissist.

Some of the things that bring about this change are as follows:

- Understanding of the four main types of narcissists you can encounter
- How to spot the unique traits that differentiate each of these narcissists
- Why they behave in this manner
- Recovery tactics to overcome their abuse

These are some of the things that play a significant role in helping you to build a better and stronger relationship between the narcissist and yourself.

There is a reason why I tag the information that I unveil in this book as revolutionary. This is mainly due to the impact it has on the lives of people that have access to this information. I have been privileged to work with various individuals going through narcissistic abuse over the years.

The Four Types of Narcissism

These are people who used the results of my research along with the various tactics in dealing with the narcissist in their lives. The feedback from these individuals has been phenomenal. Most of them mention how they have come to understand better the narcissist in their life beyond the mask they put on.

Other people mention the impact of the recovery tactics in overcoming the narcissistic abuse they receive from the narcissist. These success stories remain my inspiration in creating these books to help others.

Taking advantage of my expertise and the help I offer, I am confident that you will develop the essential skills, knowledge, and tactics that you require in overcoming the narcissistic abuse. You will also learn to live a happier life through other tactics that assist you in rebuilding your self-esteem regardless of how low it has fallen.

In my quest to help others overcome the narcissist in their life, there is a famous quote that I have rephrased to suit this purpose. I'm sure you know the saying, "Good things come to those who wait." I don't accept this phrase when dealing with narcissistic abuse. The simple reason is that every moment you waste is more time for additional damage from the narcissist.

A better saying that I adopt is, "Great things come to those who take action now." This is much closer to the truth when dealing with narcissistic abuse. Waiting for the good things to come in a narcissistic relationship is indirectly opening the gates for more problems to creep in.

Assume the narcissistic abuse as a cut. Instead of letting the cut get deeper, you must start applying medicine to heal the wound. The information you find in this book is the medicine you need for the healing process, and the sooner you learn this information, the faster you will get better.

Regardless of how long you have been receiving abuse from the narcissist, the tactics in this book are proven to yield positive results. For each chapter you complete, there is crucial information that gives you more enlightenment on the narcissist in your life. You'll start by pulling off their mask and then going deeper into their true self.

You will also learn to pick yourself up from the ground, restore your self-esteem, and go through a complete revolutionary recovery process. As long as you act on the information I provide in this book, your interaction with a narcissist will change forever.

I am not saying you won't ever have to deal with one ever again, but I promise that you will see yourself live a happier life despite their presence.

CHAPTER 1

Where Does NPD Come From?

What is Narcissism?

Narcissism refers to the act of loving oneself above others. To break it down, it involves actions that require an individual to prioritize their needs and desires above those of anyone else. Narcissism also consists of creating a barrier to keep out anyone trying to get close to you.

Narcissism is noticeable in various individuals, including friends, family, spouses, and colleagues. The spouse who shifts the blame to you when things go wrong or takes credit for everything good that happens can be a narcissist. It can also be your boss at work who exhibits the same behavior.

A narcissist may also focus on attaining and maintaining the perfect status or recognition. They work toward evoking jealousy from other individuals while showing signs of self-absorption.

A further look at narcissism shows that it is a behavior that results from Narcissistic Personality Disorder (NPD). So, what exactly is NPD?

What is Narcissistic Personality Disorder (NPD)?

As a personality disorder, NPD is a type of mental condition. This personality disorder includes various behavioral traits such as self-centeredness, inability to understand the feelings of others or a lack of empathy, and arrogance. The individual with this personality disorder–the narcissist, will usually show signs of manipulation and selfishness while being deceitful and demanding when necessary.

They crave an excess amount of admiration and attention from anyone they interact with. These traits are noticeable in their relationships with friends and family, as well as their daily interactions with other people. The psychological diagnosis of NPD also includes other aspects beyond the physical behavior.

A narcissist will usually create a false self that they adopt and put on in their interaction with others. This false self is a form of ideology that the narcissist uses in masking their insecurity and low self-esteem. Since the goal of the false self is to overcome insecurities, it is common to notice a narcissist seeking validation for their behavior from people around them.

People that show signs of NPD also find it very difficult to accept responsibility when things don't go their way. They will resort to blame-shifting and other tactics that will get another person to take the fall for the failure.

In clinical psychology and other mental health fields, the word "narcissist" isn't used to refer to just anyone. For an individual to be referred to as a "narcissist," they must meet specific requirements. These are requirements according to the Diagnostic and Statistical Manual of Mental Disorders.

Causes of NPD

There is currently no identifiable primary cause of NPD available. This makes it quite similar to other forms of personality disorders. Nonetheless, there are certain well researched theories in place to help understand some of the things that may result in NPD.

The upbringing of a child is one of the theories that are in use to try and explain the reason for NPD. In this theory, actions such as bad parenting, lack of care, excessive pampering, trauma, and abuse can lead to NPD.

Abuse and continuous acts to make a child feel worthless often have a detrimental effect on the development of a child. Such children often learn ways to survive without depending on others. In their adulthood, they adopt the belief that they can only trust themselves. As a result, they see other people around them as irrelevant.

A Narcissist's Childhood: Neglectful or Overindulgent Parents

To understand the roots of the narcissistic personality disorder in individuals, you must understand their childhood. Most narcissists often get their personality from their childhood. In the healthy development of a child, you notice that they are selfish in their actions.

A small child doesn't have an interest in your desires and doesn't even understand what they mean. Nonetheless, they are continually putting in the effort to get what they want. These actions go on until they become teenagers.

You will think they will become more understanding by this age, but nothing changes. They still engage in these selfish behaviors. Their quest to become independent from their parents is one of the self-centered actions that are common with teens.

You must understand that self-centeredness isn't the same as self-esteem. Self-esteem during development must always remain, while there must be a decline in the self-centeredness of the child. These two qualities work hand-in-hand in making the child a better person in life.

Due to their lasting self-esteem, they can shut down any unhealthy influence from others while the declining self-centeredness makes it possible for them to connect and care for others in the society and family. Since it doesn't involve placing a priority on your needs at the expense of others, self-esteem doesn't mean self-centeredness. It is merely a means to know your worth and avoid any mistreatment from others.

Through the gradual decline of the self-centeredness from childhood, they can develop the skill to view things from the perspective of others. They also learn to understand the emotions of others and show empathy. The inability of a child to show empathy is a sign of a personality disorder.

This is one of the indications of a narcissistic personality disorder. Regardless of these signs, the clinical diagnosis of narcissistic personality disorder is only possible after an individual turns 18. So, how do you determine a narcissist before this age?

There are certain things that you can notice before a clinical diagnosis that are indications of the narcissistic personality disorder. If you are looking for their manipulative tendencies,

The Four Types of Narcissism

I will advise that you forget about that for now. Before adulthood, it is impossible to develop these manipulative skills fully. The more prominent signs you should try to identify at this age include the following:

- A strong drive to come out a winner regardless of the negative effect on others
- When they get upset or receive criticism, their first response is aggression
- Their competitiveness outweighs their cooperativeness
- Prioritizing their needs over those of others
- Making others act as scapegoats, ridiculing others, threatening, and engaging in other acts of bullying
- Lying regularly to further their goals or protect their reputation
- A sense of entitlement that promotes them to demand their needs to be met regardless of current circumstances or situation
- Blame-shifting when things don't work out as expected

Parenting Styles that Promote Narcissism

In the development of a child, there is a high possibility of them growing up to become narcissists depending on how you train them. These include the indulgent, neglectful, and authoritarian parenting styles.

Neglectful Parenting Style

The neglectful parenting style is easy to identify. It is noticeable in families in which both parents work long hours without enough time to involve themselves emotionally in the lives of their children. These parents are usually incognito except in providing the basic needs that include shelter and food.

In various homes that show signs of neglectful parenting, there may be differences in the level. In some homes, the parents are unavailable to have any impact on the lives of the children once they provide the basics. In other homes, the parents still take time to impose minor restrictions such as curfews but are unable to offer parental affection or guidance to the kids.

Signs of Neglectful Parenting

There are some other signs that are clear indications of neglectful parenting in the life of a child. These include the following:

- A lack of adequate supervision
- Parents intentionally avoiding coming in contact with their children
- They have no behavioral demands or expectations from the children
- They have more significant problems to deal with that makes it difficult to focus on the children
- Absence from parent-teacher conferences and other school events
- Lack of emotional connection
- No display of affection, warmth, or love from the parents

Effects in Developing Narcissism

Neglectful parenting style has an impact on promoting narcissism in children. Due to the neglect they experience from their parents, these children can grow up with the following outcomes:

- Lack of family support that results in fear and anxiety
- They find it difficult to form attachments with others
- They lack the sense of acceptable social boundaries

Overindulgent Parenting Style

This is a parenting style in which parents are highly responsive to the needs of their children both emotionally and physically. Despite this responsiveness, they also show signs of placing low demands on the children. This lack of demands means that they will accept any form of immaturity in the behavior of the child.

They don't put in place any form of guidelines or rules that the child must follow and are usually very lax in their style of parenting. Discipline isn't a part of their techniques in training a child, but they show love and warmth, which makes them different from the neglectful parents.

They have a bond that makes them appear more like a friend to the kids than a parent. The lack of discipline from indulgent parents is because their expectations of maturity and self-control from the child are shallow.

This parenting style is noticeable in parents who engage in an overvaluation of their children. These are individuals that often objectify their children. This objectification is one of the actions that promote narcissism. The children tend to copy this idea of objectification and overvaluation from their parents.

In applying these techniques, they overvalue an individual to gain their attention and then objectify them to make them more like useful tools that they can dispose of later. When parents apply overvaluation to the child, they make them feel perfect and superior. By objectifying them, they promote feelings of worthlessness that creates low self-esteem that is noticeable in the true self of the narcissist.

Overvaluation creates a sense of entitlement in children as they grow older. They feel that they don't need to work to get things that they think they deserve. Overvaluation is also one of the actions that lead to grandiosity.

The parents continuously focus on the perfection of the child without accepting that there are also imperfections. This makes it difficult for the child to develop in a healthy manner. In their development, they grow up with two extremes, which are the hyperinflated ego and the intense feeling of worthlessness.

This lack of opportunity to develop a healthy self-image is a significant reason why they grow into a narcissistic personality. To replace this healthy self-image, the child will focus on developing an attribute to stand out. This might be intellect or appearance.

Traits of Indulgent Parenting

If you want to determine if a person is engaging in the indulgent parenting style, there are certain things you can look out for. These include the following:

- They shower their children with love and warmth
- There is a lack of discipline for most bad behaviors of the child
- Don't have too many rules to control the child
- Freedom of the child takes precedence over the child accepting responsibility
- Make significant decisions with input from the child

There is also the authoritarian parenting method that can lead to narcissism. In this method, the parents force the children to be perfect. This includes forcing them to always win and instilling toughness in the child.

Common Traits of NPD

NPD as a personality disorder has certain traits that you can attach to it. These traits appear in all narcissists regardless of the type of narcissist. Learning these traits can help you determine a narcissist before looking for more distinctive traits. These include the following:

They are Constantly Trying to Make Others Look Bad

To enhance their reputation, a narcissist will continually try to paint a bad picture of another individual. Through this action, they tend to look good at the expense of others. There are instances in which they make positive comments about other individuals if it enhances their image by association.

This is the case when you find someone that you don't like. The narcissist will make comments about how they interact excellently with that particular individual. This gives the impression that you are to blame for not getting along with the said individual.

Another rare situation in which a narcissist praises another individual is when they get a woman, they consider a "trophy" wife. Since you can't have someone as beautiful as his wife, he will exploit this situation to make you look bad.

At the slightest opportunity, they will try to show off this win.

They often spread lies about others and find it difficult to make any comment that places another individual in a positive light. Their method of destroying the image of others is often very subtle and difficult to notice. To identify this, you can listen when the narcissist is talking about another individual and ask yourself, will any of these comments make me feel good about myself?

They Get Angry When Things Don't Go Their Way

Narcissists have an unhealthy sense of entitlement. This makes them believe that everything must be done to please them. If you try to do otherwise, then they often get angry.

This unnecessary anger is crucial to the narcissists plan to regain control of a situation. Your disregard for their preferences is seen as a challenge to the control the narcissist has established. Their anger is used to intimidate, project blame, and ensure that their ego and image remains intact.

They Have an Insincere Charm

The first time you meet a narcissist, they can appear to be an extremely charming individual. As you continue to interact with them, you begin to notice that the charm is superficial. This will make them appear boastful and conceited.

They Continually Tell Lies and Exaggerate

The thing about the lies and exaggerations of a narcissist is that there is no limitation. The narcissists tell the lies and exaggerate about other people and themselves. This is often in their quest to put others down.

They try to assert their superiority over others by bragging, showing off, and looking to take credit when they don't deserve it. The narcissist has no problem using lies to discredit facts and create falsehoods in an intentional attempt to boost their self-worth and image.

They Inflict Emotional Suffering

In the victims of narcissistic abuse, it is common for most of the victims to leave the relationship without experiencing any form of physical abuse. Regardless, they still leave the relationship damaged. This is due to the emotional suffering that narcissists inflict on their victims.

They engage in forms of invalidation to keep their victims insecure, making it more difficult for them to escape the abuse. To increase the intensity of this emotional suffering, they apply gaslighting techniques to make victims take the blame for their pain.

False Projection

Image is what matters most to the narcissist. They ensure they have an image that is worthy of envy which they project to the world. This is usually in the form of the false self.

Most narcissists often appear very good in their outward appearance. This can be financially, physically, sexually, academically, religiously, or socially. Standing out in just one of these areas works for the narcissist. This doesn't stop them from improving other areas.

This image they portray to the world is one of the ways they can trigger the narcissistic supply from people around them. By evoking thoughts of admiration or love, they can get this supply. How many times have you thought about how amazing a person is without interacting with them?

The narcissist wants to receive admiration from everyone around. A more straightforward way to put it is that they want to be worshipped.

They Resort to Aggression and Denial When Criticized on their Flaws

Narcissists want others to see them as perfect. Being an ideal being is impossible. This is a fact, but it doesn't matter to the narcissist.

The narcissist will often choose either the fight or flight response when anyone decides to point out these flaws. Such actions also count as criticism and a direct attack on the ego of the narcissist.

The fight responses that the narcissist may adopt include making excuses, blame-shifting, denial, or having a temper tantrum. These responses are usually common with the overt narcissists. In the case of the covert narcissists, they typically adopt the flight responses.

The flight responses are various passive-aggressive actions such as giving the silent treatment, avoidance, and sulking resentment. In some cases, the narcissist will resort to escalation as a form of aggressiveness. This will involve them intimidating the individual to get them to back down.

They have no Respect for Boundaries or Rules

There are various actions that the narcissist takes that do not comply with the social norms that you know. They revel in these actions. They want to show their superiority by not conforming to your standards.

Putting up a barrier is how you set a limit to how much you are willing to take from others. A narcissist knows that you have these boundaries but will purposely intrude into the space behind these boundaries.

They do this to see your reaction. Don't just see it as a test; it is also a way to get their supply. The supply is complete once they get a reaction from you. It can be either a negative or positive reaction. Some actions that test these boundaries include using your belongings without permission, going back on an agreement, missing appointments, intruding in your personal space, or cutting in line.

These actions are signs of their sense of entitlement. It is a way for them to oppress those that they see as inferior to them. These are just minor cases of disrespect. Severe cases go as far as physical assault, sexual harassment, rape, and many more. Getting away with such actions fuels their sense of superiority.

There are other signs of NPD that you may notice. Most of these will be discussed further when looking at the specific traits of each type of narcissist. They include the following:

- Hijacking and dominating a conversation to make it about them
- They are jealous of the achievements of others and try to belittle these achievements
- They believe that their interaction should be limited to only those that are superior
- They want people to accept their superiority without question
- They are manipulative and exploit others to reach their goals

Is Narcissism a Survival Technique?

This is a question that goes beyond merely looking at a narcissist as that person that is out to cause damage, manipulate, and exploit others. It involves taking a deeper dive into the narcissists' mind. You can give yourself an answer to this question by comparing the false self of the narcissist to the true self.

The true self is the real person behind the narcissist, while the false self is the mask. Why would anyone decide to bury their true self so deep while allowing the world to see the false self? The only conclusion you can draw is that there is something that must be protected.

This applies to the case of the narcissist. The true self is often present while they are growing up. This is the part of the narcissist that genuinely experiences the dark side of life. The true self of the narcissist is usually the vulnerable part of the narcissist.

The true self of the narcissist often has low self-esteem, which can result from a feeling of worthlessness, objectification by parents, or starvation of love, and abuse. The problem with this true self is the fact that it feels pain. The individual will also go through periods of self-doubt.

For an ordinary individual, overcoming this childhood trauma will involve healing this true self. For the narcissist, they think to themselves, "Why should I have to go through this sort of pain?" This can seem like a typical response until you understand the consequence.

The consequence of this is that the individual decides that they don't want to feel this sort of pain henceforth. To make this possible means that the true self has to go. This means creating a new persona, which is the false self. The key trait of this false self is a lack of vulnerability.

This is to ensure that there is no repeat of what happened to the true self. There is a reason why it is so easy for the false self to take over. This is because the true self is much too weak to fight back.

It is also an acceptance to prevent it from disappearing. You will notice that there are certain instances when the narcissist loses their ability to function normally. This is notable in communal narcissists who have more difficulty keeping up their facade.

This is what the narcissist tries to avoid. Through the invulnerability of the false self, you notice a change in the narcissistic child. The child becomes immune to any form of abuse such as sadism, indifference, smothering, or manipulation from caretakers or parents.

Another function of this false self is to change how people act toward the individual. It works to prevent abuse from others while evoking better treatment from others. By understanding this comparison between the false self and true self, there is only one conclusion you can draw.

Despite your inability to accept the narcissist for his/her actions, there is a reason for these actions. The narcissistic personality they develop is usually an unintentional outcome of their need to protect themselves from hurt and pain. It is a survival technique they come up with through the creation of the false self.

Although this may be the outcome of a survival technique, the narcissist can become self-aware of this and learn to love their false self.

CHAPTER 2

What Really Goes Through a Narcissists Mind?

Living in Their Little World

Understanding how the mind of a narcissist works requires you to accept that how you see the world differs from the narcissists' view. Narcissists often have a little world of their own in which they are the sun, and every other thing revolves around them. How do narcissists attain this conceited view of the world?

A closer look at the life of the narcissist can help in understanding what goes on in their mind. This is what lies beyond the absence of empathy, entitlement, arrogance, manipulation, and grandiosity that they display to the world. In dealing with a narcissist, being sympathetic can help you get over most of their antics without letting it damage you.

The first thing you have to understand about the narcissist is that the behaviors and traits they display to the world create a mask that hides a unique side of the narcissist. This is a more vulnerable side that the narcissist feels will change how the world looks at them. A distinct feature of the hidden side of the narcissist is low self-esteem.

This is ironic since narcissists often leave their victim in a state of low self-esteem. Is this simply a coincidence or a way to do onto others what has been done to them? Unless you are a narcissist, you may never know the answer to this.

One thing we do know is that the various narcissistic traits are defense mechanisms to prevent any form of humiliation or shame. It is a clear depiction of attack as the best form of defense.

From childhood, most narcissists experience feelings of inadequacy, weakness, and unworthiness. This paints a picture that differs from the entitled and spoiled child they become due to overindulgent parents. This is one of the reasons a narcissist will continually seek ways to develop personal qualities that make them stand out.

Deciphering the world of the narcissist will lead to a realization that their need for attention and sense of entitlement are essential in compensating for their lack thereof. These things they compensate for include the lack of support, warmth, and validation while growing up.

The Four Types of Narcissism

The lack of these essential feelings sinks their self-esteem. The attitude and demeanor they develop later in life is a way of them disproving this truth. They are forcefully feeding themselves lies that in comparison to other individuals, they are more deserving of these feelings.

To validate these claims, they implement various tactics that result in the devaluation of other individuals. These actions include deceit, ridicule, and other antisocial behaviors. While it is at the expense of others, they do end up feeling better about who they are at the moment.

The unconscious actions become their response to their inability to gain acceptance, love, and other forms of positive feelings from their parents or guardians. The world of the narcissist shows its imperfection in the high probability of the narcissist sinking into depression.

Due to their actions such as deceit, devaluation, and discard of individuals, they often end up alone. The loneliness is a trigger that causes their hidden emotions to resurface suddenly. The shame, humiliation, abandonment, and emptiness that are hidden deep within their psyche suddenly overwhelm them.

This is noticeable in situations where a victim starts to see through the narcissist and decides to leave the relationship.

They resort to the narcissistic rage to try to regain control of their victims. When this tactic fails to yield positive results, it gives room for depression in the life of the narcissist.

Depression in the world of the narcissist is an indication that their façade and mask has been unsuccessful in attaining their innermost desires. These desires are the things that were missing during their childhood. This is the positive acknowledgment of their parents, which they try to get from others.

In the adult narcissist, the intensity of their feelings of abandonment, humiliation, and shame is more intense. They are unable to make any behavioral change to combat this depression since their narcissistic personality depends on failed systems they put in place.

Adding Gas to the Fire

Assume the narcissistic personality to be the fire, what keeps this fire burning? Do narcissists have an inner fuel or is there an external factor that plays a role in maintaining the personality?

How Do They Get Their Fuel?

The fuel that the narcissist requires is available in the form of admiration, praise, attention, or recognition. These are the various positive cues that they get both in verbal and nonverbal forms. You can liken it to the positive remarks and compliments that you get for a specific action or those you offer when trying to reinforce a behavior.

Unlike in the case of regular people who want this form of admiration or attention in small amounts from time to time, a narcissist wants it in large quantities at all times. They need the admiration, attention, affirmation, and praise because it serves as their fuel.

Due to their inflated ego, they are not okay with the little quantities that satisfy others. They are willing to go to any extent to get these positive cues out of other individuals.

A term that defines the narcissists' fuel is the "Narcissistic Supply." This encompasses the various forms through which narcissists derive their fuel. The multiple characteristics of the narcissists' false self, such as their charm, success, and intelligence are essential in generating this fuel from others.

In obtaining their supply, the narcissist will usually have a trigger and a source. The source refers to the individual responsible for producing the narcissistic supply. The trigger defines the object or person that prompts the source to provide this supply. To get the source into action, the trigger will often offer a form of information such as notoriety of the narcissist, which will shift the attention of the source to the narcissist.

How do They Leave Their Victims?

Anyone unlucky to have a close connection with a narcissist often ends up as a victim of narcissistic abuse. The narcissist in your life can be a parent, spouse, or significant other in a relationship. These are individuals that have access to your daily life.

Although you end up as a victim, it is often difficult to know this until you sever the connection with the narcissist. It is during the time after leaving the narcissist that the signs of victimization become noticeable. The lack of empathy in narcissists implies that there is no limit to the extent of the damage.

In their bid to obtain supply, the narcissist will suck you empty. They prey on your emotions and go as far as leaving their victims financially troubled, lonely, and out of their job.

With some kinds of narcissists, they take this a step further by chipping at the personality and self-esteem of the victims.

How do Narcissists Exhibit Dependency?

While they don't form any deep relationship with others, narcissists are still dependent on others for their survival. This dependency is essential in getting the narcissistic supply. The dependence of the narcissist is deep-rooted in their personality.

Failure to get a narcissistic supply can make the narcissist feel like they are undergoing torture. This is a significant reason why they usually dislike a victim deciding to leave on their own and always look for a replacement before getting into the discard phase.

How Do They Gain and Maintain Control?

Gaining total control of an individual is no small feat. Regardless, narcissists do it smoothly and efficiently. This is possible through years of practice and engaging in this unhealthy act. The various actions the narcissist will take to gain control include manipulation, trickery, deceit, and cajoling.

In certain situations, narcissists will resort to physical violence to maintain the control they gain. The action they take depends on what they intend to achieve.

Physical violence is usually a typical response when there is a narcissistic injury. The narcissistic injury refers to a situation in which there is a move to disrupt their control and power. The response to the potential disruption is often a narcissistic rage.

Another reason why a narcissist may resort to physical violence is to gain control over their victim through fear. This is when they determine that manipulation won't be enough to attain full control.

Getting a New Source

There are animals like the vampire bat and lamprey that are known to suck the blood from other animals. Narcissists act similarly. The only noticeable difference is the fact that narcissists feed off your emotions and not your blood.

Since the emotions of an individual are not infinite, there is usually a need to look for a new host from time to time. They perform their search while still feeding off the current host.

The Four Types of Narcissism

This is to ensure that they are continuously receiving their supply.

There are times when the narcissist will leave a victim despite still having a lot of emotions to offer. This is common when they find a source that will provide more supply than they currently enjoy. The lack of closure and sudden discard weighs heavily on the mind of the victims, leaving them emotionally damaged.

To bait their supply, narcissists do their best to make them believe that they are friends. They know that control and manipulation are more effective on individuals that see them as trusted friends. The intelligence, charm, and friendliness they showcase during a first meeting are to leave an excellent first impression on their potential source.

That means as a source of supply; your potential replacement is likely a part of the individuals that your narcissistic partner keeps as friends. This individual will start showing up more often when you start declining the demands of the narcissist. If you consistently take actions that result in the narcissist putting in more work to get their supply, they will quickly shift to the discard phase.

Why do Narcissists often End up with Past Victims?

It is common to find out that individuals that were once in a narcissistic relationship usually end up with another narcissist. The reason for this is that they have low confidence and self-esteem, making them the perfect targets for the narcissist.

In addition to these, there are sure signs that these victims exhibit that make them more appealing to the narcissists. Due to the conditioning they undergo in their past relationship, these individuals avoid any form of conflict. The ideas of rational thinking and proper decision-making are also alien to these individuals, and this makes them easy to manipulate.

With all these traits, the icing on the cake comes in how they provide the narcissistic supply. This is one of the side effects of their past narcissistic relationship.

While the narcissist appeals to these victims using their charm, they start detecting these traits.

Is the Source Limited to Providing Emotional Needs?

A common misunderstanding is that the narcissist is limited to drawing only emotions from the victims. If you take time to look at various victims of narcissistic abuse, they are often in financial difficulties after the relationship with the narcissist.

This shows that nothing is ever enough for the narcissist. They are willing to take everything that can offer their supply. Their sense of entitlement leads them to believe that the source must give them everything they want. Finding a narcissist working fewer hours is typical. They may also move from one job to another frequently.

Does Negativity Count Toward the Narcissistic Supply?

Narcissists are out for attention. The attention that you give to others can be either positive or negative. These are all acceptable as a form of supply.

The narcissist wants to be the center of attention. Approval, fear, notoriety, applause, fame, and adulation are all forms of attention which the narcissist craves.

The narcissist is all about spreading influence to get their supply. The supply focuses on the reaction they can elicit from an individual. The narcissist will manipulate and confront an individual to ensure that they assert their control.

Narcissists and Past Sources

If you are lucky to observe the relationship between a narcissist and his/her victim come to an end, it will be easy to assume that there is an enmity between both parties. Does the narcissist see victims as enemies? No, they don't.

To the narcissist, their victims are nothing more than their sources. If as a victim, you see the narcissist as an enemy, then you are merely acting as a source. This will provoke negative emotions that the narcissist willingly accepts.

Nonetheless, narcissists do their best not to burn down old bridges. This means that they leave their victims in a state in which their return will overjoy them. This is how good they are at spreading their influence over the life of a victim.

Regardless of what state they leave their past sources, it is often a win-win for the narcissist. Both joy and hate provide them with their supply. Therefore, victims must learn to act indifferent toward the narcissist. This is one of the few things that shut down the narcissist.

Some of the Things that Scares the Narcissist

Commitment to a Relationship

Since a relationship commitment means that you need to expose yourself and vulnerabilities to your partner, this is one of the things narcissists avoid. This lack of commitment is usually noticeable in victims of narcissistic abuse.

These individuals usually experience an emotional mismatch and starvation of love. The narcissist also chooses to objectify their partners to avoid commitment. This is to protect their secrets.

Self-Reflection

The initial goal of creating the false self is to prevent the narcissist from coming to terms with their insecurities and flaws. Engaging in self-reflection will cause them to come to terms with the true self. This is the opposite of the narcissists need to see themselves as perfect.

Receiving Insults

Insults can mean receiving criticism. Noticeable in the way they react, narcissists don't like to be insulted. Despite how quick they are to dish it out to others; it is something that genuinely scares them.

The reason for this is that criticism tends to expose the true self of the narcissist. This is something the narcissist will never accept.

Shame

In a later chapter, you will learn that narcissists lack a sense of shame. This doesn't imply that they don't feel it, but it means it doesn't weigh them much. The sort of shame that affects narcissist is being seen as unworthy in society or being beneath others.

Lack of Attention

Narcissists want to be noticed. It is how they get their supply and attract a new source. One of the few things that scare them is going through a place completely unnoticed. This can involve people ignoring anything they try to do within that period.

It is a sign that they are unable to evoke a reaction from these individuals, which results in a lack of supply for the narcissist.

Having Their Lies Exposed

Nothing is worse than being called out on your lies. In your bid to increase your appeal, you might often sneak in one or two lies into a conversation. Narcissists also do this. The difference is that in everything they say to boost their appeal, there is little truth.

Continually lying to people means that there is a possibility of getting called out on one of these lies soon. Narcissists dread such a fate.

Showing Gratitude

Narcissists don't want to accept that you were of any help to them. This is what it means when they decide to say thank you for an act. Gratitude is a sign that they were relying on you.

CHAPTER 3

5 Incredibly Destructive Tactics Narcissists Will Use to Bring You Down

The actions the narcissists take are all in preparation for when you decide to leave them. They know that their actions and behaviors don't make sense, so how can they get you to stay? These are what the destructive tactics of the narcissist are in place to achieve.

These tactics are used to bring down the victims making it difficult for them to leave the narcissistic relationship. Some tactics also play a role in attracting you to the narcissist.

Each tactic in the arsenal of the narcissist has a unique function. There is a tactic for blame-shifting, alienating you from friends and family, destroying your self-esteem, protecting the narcissist, and throwing you out in the end. Understanding these tactics can help in protecting yourself.

False Self, True Self

How did the narcissist in your life gain your affection? How did you become another source of narcissistic supply? A simple answer to this is the false self, true self tactic of the narcissist.

You can refer to the false self as a mask, but it also serves as an armor for the narcissist. The narcissist often goes through a degree of abuse as a child. The pain that they receive at this point in life is a driving factor in the development of the false sense.

They conclude that their emotions and sensitivity play a role in their vulnerability. Creating a false self is their answer to stopping the hurt and pain that they experience at a young age. Without anyone to point out the flaws in their thinking, they choose to lock down their emotions.

The false self is their way of announcing to the world that they don't deserve the pain and hurt being inflicted on them. The intention they have when creating this mask is to ensure that people change the way they treat them.

In the life of the narcissist, one function of the false self is to emulate the true self. The false self is capable of replicating various emotions to assist in deceiving their victims. To achieve a perfect emulation of emotions, the narcissist observes and records what goes on around.

What is the consequence of a specific phrase? What is the reaction to this action? These are some of the things the narcissist looks out for. They mentally create a data book of these observations.

Using the information from this mental data book, the false self is ready to reproduce an image close to the true self. It produces an emotional behavior that is difficult to see through, regardless of the deceit behind it.

Another function is reinterpretation. We all know that narcissists lack empathy and reactions that are normal with others. So, why do they think otherwise?

This is what the false self does by reinterpretation. They reinterpret any form of discomfort they feel as their sign of compassion and empathy. Through this compassion, they understand that they will get acknowledgment from society. This is one way for them to obtain their supply.

In most cases in which the true self of the narcissist is observable from time to time, they are still not full-fledged narcissists. This means that while they may be narcissistic in their personality and behavior, under the strict psychiatric conditions, they are not wholly narcissistic.

The Four Types of Narcissism

Idealization, Devaluation, Discard

Narcissists usually look for someone to serve as their narcissistic supply in their everyday life. To get this supply, they search for an individual who they rope in. How do they do this?

By implementing the idealization, devaluation, and discard tactic, the narcissist can obtain narcissistic supply. This tactic involves moving through three different phases to achieve the result the narcissist desires. The idealization, devaluation, and discard are the first, second, and third phases, respectively.

The tactic begins with the idealization phase. This is during the period you meet the narcissist. This phase involves the narcissist treating you right, making you feel like you're on top of the world, and love-bombing you.

These are all the things that make the narcissist seem like a perfect match. The regular attention you receive is often enough to get you into their trap. The flattery, calls, and effort they put into being with you most times all promote their love-bombing technique.

This is a mask that the narcissist puts on to hide their true intentions. They take off this mask as soon as they get into the devaluation phase. Once this mask is off, you will start noticing a side of the narcissist that was impossible to identify during the idealization phase.

The narcissist will shift to this phase when they determine that you have bought into the idea of the relationship. It is during this period that you start receiving negative comments from the narcissist, cold treatment, and stonewalling. The narcissist will find ways to pull you down by retracting the positive remarks and flattery they used in gaining your attention during the initial stage.

If you try to react, the narcissist will implement the gaslighting technique, so you begin to self-doubt. In a narcissistic relationship, the first time this happens is often the best time to get out of the relationship. Most individuals miss this opportunity because there will be a period during which the narcissist makes a convincing argument of the reason for the abuse through blame-shifting and gaslighting.

If you are unlucky to fall for this trick, then you have set yourself up for a continuous cycle through the idealization and devaluation phases during the relationship. As the cycle continues, they keep increasing the severity of the abuse to know your limits.

The Four Types of Narcissism

The final phase is the discard phase. This is when the narcissist throws you out of their life to give room for their new supply. It is the step they take when they feel you no longer meet the requirements of serving as their narcissistic supply.

Most cases in which narcissists discard their victims, it is often due to the victim starting to make demands and set healthy boundaries. A narcissist believes that their victim must give in to all their needs without question. Failure to do this means that the individual is no longer a perfect supply source.

The discard phase is often the most damaging phase of the three. This is because the narcissist will do their best to instill a feeling of worthlessness and a lack of closure when discarding. They also humiliate and demean these individuals.

They can exhibit more violent actions toward their victim, leave without any final words, or show off a new partner. All these actions are in a bid to make sure you will always remember them. This is what makes it challenging to recover from the narcissistic abuse even after the relationship.

In cases when you leave the relationship early or hold on until the discard phase, narcissists will also implement a tactic known as hoovering. It is a tactic through which the narcissist gets back into your life to discard you again in a worse manner. It is through this tactic that narcissists display their darkest side.

Gaslighting

For anyone who regularly interacts with a narcissist, it is common for the narcissist to have frequent abusive outbursts. During the initial stages of the interaction, your reaction to these outbursts is quite reasonable from your perspective. Regardless, you suddenly start to wonder if you are overreacting.

Why is this so? Through the gaslighting tactics, a narcissist will make you question your reactions. The purpose of this tactic is to make it seem like the abuse didn't occur in the first place and make it easier for the narcissist to manipulate an individual.

As a victim of the gaslighting technique, you may begin to develop a form of self-doubt in how you interpret various situations. This self-doubt is what the narcissist preys on to keep you in the relationship. As a result of this self-doubt, the narcissist can alter your perception of an event and cause you to become dependent on them.

To bring you down, the goal of the gaslighting tactic is to help the narcissist be in control. To achieve this goal, there are specific steps that he/she will often take. These are as follows:

Getting the Victim on the Defensive

To do this, the narcissist will go on the offensive. The various actions that help them stay on the offensive include lying, denial, and exaggerating a situation. A phrase like "I didn't make that statement" is a form of denial that puts you on the defensive.

Repeating the Lies

When a narcissist continues to repeat a lie, it starts to become the truth for everyone. This is also a necessary step that always puts you on the defensive while they can control both the relationship and conversations you have.

Misdirection and Escalation

The narcissist always wants to be right. Therefore, they can't let anyone find out their lies or any evidence that makes them out as the abuser. To do this, they perform actions that escalate a situation or engage in misdirection.

To escalate the situation, you can expect an increase in the abusive outbursts you experience. To misdirect, they make things more confusing by coming up with new false accusations and denying any proof you might have come across. These false claims do well to make you forget some essential facts.

Get You to Back Down

As soon as you start having second thoughts about your reality and perception, you slowly begin to back down. You begin to lose hope and resign yourself into accepting your current situation. This is one of the effects of the constant offensive stance that the narcissist adopts during the gaslighting process.

Make You Codependent

The focus of a narcissist engaging in gaslighting is to gain control. Once they are in control, you become a puppet in their show. To create the perfect puppet, they cause you to become co-dependent.

Now that you have become reliant on the narcissist both psychologically and emotionally, you develop a form of vulnerability and fear. You are vulnerable in the sense that the narcissist is now responsible for providing the feeling of safety, acceptance, respect, and security that you need. Your fear is due to the fact that the narcissist can easily prevent your access to these essential feelings.

A Sense of Remorse

It is easier to accept a person when you think they have reflected over their actions and feel a sense of remorse. This is an art that narcissists can pull out of their arsenal during gaslighting. You suddenly start experiencing remorseful actions such as kindness and mildness from your abuser.

Prior to these actions, you should have begun to develop some protective traits that make it difficult for you to give in to the narcissist. These remorseful actions are superficial and intended to pull down this wall with ease. Once you start noticing these positive changes that seem so real, you assume that there is no need for these walls any longer.

These positive actions only last a short time. This is the interval that the narcissist utilizes in making you careless. Once you become lax in your defenses, your abuser implements the gaslighting tactic again.

Assume the Role of a Puppeteer

As I mentioned earlier, gaslighting is a technique to help the narcissist be in control. A puppeteer is skilled at controlling more than one puppet, so don't be surprised if the narcissist is in control of the actions of your friends and family toward you.

The lies that make you feel self-doubt, insecurity, and fear are essential in keeping you as a puppet. That is why the gaslighting tactic requires the narcissist to continually tell numerous lies to ensure you remain in this state.

Triangulation

Triangulation is a common tactic that a narcissist will use when they intend to bring you down. This is a tool that makes it easy for a narcissist to manipulate and control your emotions. The goal of this tactic is to make you get jealous while the narcissist appears to be more desirable.

To do this, they will bring in a third party. This third party can be a single individual or a group of people. They create a triangle that consists of the narcissist, yourself, and the third party.

The Four Types of Narcissism

By including this group or individual, you get the feeling that there are lots of other people working on getting the narcissist out of your grip. Therefore, you decide to fight for the narcissist and come out as the one who is liked more. It is a form of competition that will make the narcissist seem more valuable.

In truth, there are two functions of the third party in this triangle. The first is to act as a tool that will elicit feelings of jealousy from you. The second reason why a narcissist will introduce a third party is to replace you. They prepare this individual to take over your role as soon as they enter into the discard phase with you.

During the triangulation tactic, there will be a lot of manipulation from the narcissist without your knowledge. They often implement this tactic along with the smear campaign. The smear campaign is necessary for the narcissist to become more appealing to the new target.

They might tell lies like you being abusive and crazy to their new victim. On the other hand, you will receive compliments from the narcissist when you are alone. This is what drives you to fight for their attention during the triangulation.

Smear Campaigns

When you finally get an opening to stop interacting with the narcissist in your life, don't expect them to let you go that easy. They will usually try to bring you down by engaging in a smear campaign. This is a tactic that can ruin your reputation and relationships with friends, family, colleagues, and neighbors.

The smear campaign is often in a bid to prevent you from exposing the unpleasant side of the narcissist that you have come to know. As a result of this tactic, the narcissist can maintain his/her appearance as a perfect individual to others. The smear campaign involves the narcissist coming up with exaggerated lies that they tell to the ones that matter the most to you.

Since the narcissist then appears as the victim, these individuals then take his/her side. To prevent you from spreading their insecurities and exposing them to shame, you can expect the narcissist to engage in a smear campaign involving:

The Four Types of Narcissism

Your Family

For every individual, your family members are always willing to offer their support when you are at your low. The narcissist knows this, so they find a way to prevent it. They do this by telling you lies about your family while also speaking lies to your family about you.

As a result of their actions, you hold a grudge against your family members while they also hold a grudge against you. Amidst the misunderstanding between both parties, the only winner is the narcissist who retains your trust and that of your family. In the end, you are unable to get the crucial support you need from your family members if you need to get out of the relationship and have to rely more on the narcissist.

Your Workplace

If there is a smear campaign involving your colleagues, it is often to make it difficult for you to focus on your work. For individuals who are dealing with a narcissist parent, going no contact may cause them to use this tactic. They can go as far as reaching out to your colleagues or boss to tell them lies about you to retain control.

If your spouse is the narcissist in your life, then it won't be unusual to have them making negative comments about your work. They might decide to spread lies about you to your boss or label your boss as a narcissist, so it creates a rift.

These actions are essential to the narcissist who wants to have the most influence and authority over you. A job is one of the few things that pose a threat to the control they have; hence, the need to destroy it.

Court Proceedings

In a relationship with a narcissist spouse, a divorce may seem like the final step to escape. Regardless, the smear campaign can also be applied in this situation. You can expect to be involved in a back and forth due to the narcissist changing their demands often.

To get the upper hand, they are willing to expose any of your medical report that gives them an unfair advantage.

Your Friends

Getting you away from your friends is another way for the narcissist to come out as the winner. Telling their lies to your friends can help them get what they want. Not all your friends will accept the things they say, but some of them will.

The Four Types of Narcissism

They are your friends, why should they believe these lies about you? This is a simple thought that makes you avoid contact with these friends. In other cases, you may decide to take your frustration out on the narcissist in your life.

Regardless of the action you take, the only thing you achieve is establishing the lies of the narcissist as the truth.

Getting out of the smear campaign as the winner, there are some actions you can take. These include the following:

- Find an excellent therapist or people that will support you
- Avoid contact with the narcissist if possible
- Prepare yourself for the role of the abuser when the narcissist tells the story

CHAPTER 4

The Grandiose Narcissist

Grandiose narcissists are those that believe their reality of being what they say it is. They believe so much that what they say is true and often go the distance to make others believe it too. They are incredibly efficient in the use of gaslighting to get an individual to question their own reality or if the narcissist's reality is the truth.

In the development of the grandiose personality, there is often a link with the childhood of these type of narcissists. Overindulgent parenting is the root cause of the grandiosity they exhibit. This makes them different from the other form of narcissist known as the vulnerable narcissist.

The vulnerable narcissist is often the result from a form of parenting that you can tag as neglectful. The overindulgent parenting in grandiose narcissists implies that their parents get them to think and accept that they are entitled and superior to others. This parenting style is also noticeable in their unwillingness to caution their children anytime they pull down the boundaries that other children have out in place.

You can expect these parents to pamper the child excessively while showing signs of indifference even when the child does wrong. If you observe other parents that raise their kids right, not only do they caution their child, they also show signs of remorse and empathy. These are indications that they hold themselves accountable for the wrongdoing and behaviors of the child.

As adults, grandiose narcissists are more likely to not bother themselves with how others see them. This is very much unlike how other narcissists behave. In their way of thinking, the grandiose narcissist recognizes his/her greatness without needing to hear it from anyone else.

This self-acknowledgment is one of the reasons why they can look at others with a dismissive attitude. The look that you can translate to the narcissist saying, "I am superior, and you are inferior to me." This is one of the behaviors that irritate anyone they have a relationship with.

While other narcissists will try to enhance their image by putting down others, the grandiose narcissist doesn't feel the need to do so. They see it as an unnecessary effort since they believe there was never any comparison in the first place.

They can appear to be oblivious since they are usually unaware of how their behavior or actions affect or impact the lives of others.

Key Traits and Behaviors

In identifying a grandiose narcissist, the big five personality traits help in understanding them better. In addition to some of these traits, other behaviors can assist in understanding the grandiose narcissist. These include the following:

They Have Low Neuroticism

Neuroticism is a way to describe the emotional stability of an individual. In measuring neuroticism, the scale ranges from low to high neuroticism. On this scale, the grandiose narcissist falls on the low neuroticism range.

This trait indicates that the grandiose narcissist is an individual with excellent emotional stability. They are less likely to jump into a fit of rage or show any signs of anxiousness, moodiness, or irritability. This means that they handle stressful situations very well. Nonetheless, there are times when they lose this calmness, especially when they are deprived of their supply.

The Four Types of Narcissism

If you are in a relationship with a grandiose narcissist, you will notice that it is challenging to find them feeling sad or showing any hint of depression. They rarely worry about anything and appear relaxed on most occasions.

They Exhibit High Extroversion

As extroverts, the grandiose narcissist finds it relatively easy to make friends. Their narcissistic personality flourishes in situations where they can socialize with other individuals. You will find them striking a conversation with anyone they meet with ease.

Like most of the other types of narcissists, the grandiose narcissist also enjoys it when they have the attention of everyone in a gathering. On most occasions, the grandiose narcissist will speak before considering the consequences of what they have said.

They Have a Low Agreeableness

The agreeableness of a person describes their disposition toward others. Are they likely to show affection, trust, or kindness to others? These are the questions it answers.

On this scale, the grandiose narcissist scores low. This means that your problems and feelings don't matter to them. It is easy to consider this as a lack of empathy in the grandiose narcissist.

They tend to show an uncooperative attitude by behaving stubbornly and competitively towards others. The little interest they show in others, or lack of it often appears to be a dismissive attitude toward others.

They Are Manipulative

Like other narcissists, manipulation is one of the critical traits of the grandiose narcissist. They engage in the act of manipulation to get others to do what they want or impose their views on others.

Seeing others as nothing more than an object, they believe that they should be in control of how they act and their reactions at certain times. This is how they get their supply. The idea of objectifying others makes it possible for narcissists to engage in manipulation without bothering about the consequences.

Exaggerated Sense of Self-Importance

The grandiose narcissist has a complete belief in their superiority over others. This can make them have an inflated sense of self-importance. They assume that other individuals care for them more than they actually do.

They Try to Dominate

To match their sense of superiority, grandiose narcissists are always looking for ways to become the dominant figure anywhere they find themselves. This means climbing the hierarchy to get to the top.

This can be the hierarchy in an organization, community, or family. It is this quest to dominate that promotes the competitive nature of the grandiose narcissist. Unlike other individuals that are comfortable moving up the hierarchy based on their performance, grandiose narcissists don't want to spend that much time.

They seek out the shortest route possible to achieve this ascension. It can be through exploitation, lying, or cheating. It is not uncommon for them to make use of their charm and implement seduction in attaining their goal.

They Appear to be Self-Sufficient

Taking into consideration their sense of superiority, it is easy to see a grandiose narcissist being self-sufficient. This means they act in a manner that indicates that they don't need anyone else to survive.

The signs of self-sufficiency in grandiose narcissism is usually an egocentric self-sufficiency. This means that they are selfish in their actions and don't account for the desires of others when taking any action.

Self-sufficiency can also explain why the grandiose narcissist is sometimes comfortable being alone especially when he/she considers those around to be inferior.

CHAPTER 5

The Malignant Narcissist

Malignant narcissists share some similarities with the grandiose narcissist. This is noticeable in their feeling of superiority, zero empathy, and the need for attention. The unique trait of the malignant narcissist is the severity of their narcissistic characteristics. Another factor that differentiates the malignant narcissist from others is the fact that it is not recognized in the Diagnostic and Statistical Manual of Mental Disorders (DSM-V).

Malignant narcissists, in addition to the narcissistic personality disorder, also shows signs of other forms of personality disorders. This includes antisocial personality disorder. They will also exhibit sadism, aggression, and paranoia.

The way malignant narcissists think can make them a danger to society. This includes their interactions with employees, family, loved ones, colleagues, dependents, etc. They often take actions and decisions that can be hurtful to others.

It is common for malignant narcissists to engage in splitting. The term "splitting" in psychology, refers to the inability of an individual to combine both good and evil in a single entity. They accept that one can be either good or evil with no possibility of falling between these two extremes.

In the daily interaction with a malignant narcissist, it is common to tread lightly. This often involves taking actions to soothe the ego of the narcissist and avoiding any form of criticism. The simplest things can cause an abusive outburst from the malignant narcissist.

An individual that voices a different opinion from what the malignant narcissist proposes will trigger the need for the narcissist to humiliate or lash out at them. Any form of criticism is seen as an attack to expose their true self.

They will often try to twist their reality by telling lies. If you attempt to counter these lies with facts or the truth, they get angry and resort to various tactics like gaslighting to bring you down. Since they can easily connect with other individuals, their behavior is often the reason why it is easy for them to hurt others in their relationship.

In addition to the hypersensitivity and aggression they exhibit, other factors that cause pain for others include paranoia and lack of empathy in these narcissists. If you assume that a malignant narcissist is a petty, angry, jealous, and hateful individual, then you aren't far from the truth.

They are willing to go to any extent to achieve their goals. This includes going as far as exhibiting selflessness in their actions.

In identifying what type of narcissist you are dealing with, there is often a need to seek professional help. Regardless, certain traits can help you determine if you are with a malignant narcissist.

Key Traits and Behaviors

Some of the traits and behaviors that you can associate with a malignant narcissist are given below. It is common to find a few characteristics that you can associate with other forms of narcissism, but the severity of these traits often differs for each group.

They Are Sadistic Individuals

What you notice during your time with a malignant narcissist is the pleasure they derive anytime they get the opportunity to cause suffering or pain on another individual. This is a trait that you can't overlook in these individuals. Like everything with the narcissist, this action is essential in gaining and maintaining control of their victims.

There are various ways to identify the sadistic side of a narcissist. You can notice it in how they react to violence both on TV and in real life. In real-life situations, you should carefully observe how they treat animals. This is often in the form of physical abuse that they may inflict or how they treat injured animals.

This cruelty further develops into emotional and verbal abuse of individuals. In this case, you can refer to the narcissist as an everyday sadist. This implies that the narcissist is happy to take part in the process of inflicting pain in whatever form.

Unlike "everyday" sadism that is a clear depiction of malignant narcissists, you may also stumble upon a vicarious sadist. These are individuals who don't actively participate in inflicting pain on others but usually enjoy watching others in pain.

They are Manipulative

Understanding the manipulative tendencies of a malignant narcissist is essential in identifying them better. As humans, it is quite common to engage in a bit of manipulation. This is when we find ourselves in a situation that we can use to our benefit. It is similar to the actions of other narcissists who see themselves as opportunists.

This differs from the manipulative actions of a malignant narcissist. The behavior of the malignant narcissist involves engaging in manipulation at all times. This means that they manipulate when they find an opportunity and also create their opportunities.

To create these opportunities, they engage in tactics like gaslighting. This is a tactic that causes self-doubt and confusion in their victim. Once these vulnerabilities are in place, it is much simpler to manipulate their victims.

Cutting ties with a malignant narcissist is more difficult since one of the side effects of manipulation is minimal free will. Following the constant use of these manipulative actions, they are more efficient in gaining control of their victims.

Their Feeling of Empathy is Nonexistent

If you argue that this is a trait that all narcissists possess, then you would be correct. Nonetheless, there must be a way to classify the feelings of empathy. This is what differentiates you from the narcissist.

Using a spectrum to indicate this difference, then the malignant narcissist will fall on the extreme with zero empathy. This means that while you may feel pain, they don't. For this reason, they can go on inflicting pain on others without feeling any remorse that will cause them to stop.

You can notice this lack of empathy when you decide to confront a malignant narcissist. Consider a situation in which the narcissist has an abusive outburst for no justifiable reason. You approach the narcissist, have a conversation, and you end it reflecting on your actions.

In addition to their manipulative trait, the lack of remorse from the narcissist will make blame-shifting a lot easier. You suddenly accept the fact that your actions are the reason for the outburst.

An Unhealthy Sense of Superiority

In the perception of the malignant narcissist, you are nothing. On the other hand, they see themselves as everything. They believe they are superior to everyone in all areas.

A simple way to define this is a delusion of grandeur. This drives them to exaggerate their importance, intelligence, and attractiveness with respect to that of others. In their understanding, someone as superior as they are should only associate with others that match this superiority. This causes them to label others as being inferior and looking down on them.

A sense of entitlement also develops from this feeling of superiority. A malignant narcissist will expect you to provide them with a birthday treatment every day.

They are Paranoid

In the case of the malignant narcissist, everything is extreme. The same applies to their feelings of paranoia. They adopt the stance that the world is against them.

Taking this stance gets them to over-analyze every situation and remain suspicious of everyone. The result of this paranoia is a narcissist who doesn't place his/her trust in any individual. Simply bumping into a narcissist while hurrying to catch the last bus will be misinterpreted as an intentional act to steal their wallet or get them hurt.

This paranoia is often what drives the manipulative tendencies of a malignant narcissist. For fear of an individual commenting or taking any action that won't be to their benefit, they tend to manipulate the actions of that individual. Knowing that they manipulate others, they engage in projection and assume that everyone acts similarly.

They Exhibit Antisocial Behaviors

In addition to other characteristics of malignant narcissism, this category of narcissists also exhibits antisocial personality disorder (APD) (Raypole & Leng, 2019). Some of the easily identifiable antisocial behaviors that you can expect include emotional abuse, manipulation, aggression, stealing, disregard for the safety, lying, and deceit.

They are Envious of Others

Although a narcissist wants a lot of things, it is difficult for them to get all these wants. Therefore, they get envious when they come across someone that possesses these things they want. This might be a physical possession, success, or a unique trait.

If you are unlucky to have a possession that the malignant narcissist desires, they will do everything in their power to make it seem insignificant. This may be by basing your ownership on the item on luck rather than hard work.

In a case where you are receiving accolades for your success, they can go to the extent of spreading rumors that you are a cheat. They do not show happiness for the success of others but will be ecstatic when you fail.

They are Extremely Charming Individuals

Although this is only noticeable during the initial stages of your interaction with a malignant narcissist, they are charming. This is how they get your attention and appear attractive. This charm will involve giving compliments, gifts, and telling you about their achievements. They will offer everything they know you want to hear.

This is the bait they use to get you on the hook. They are all lies that are intended to get you to lower your guard. The charm will remain in effect until you put down your guard and become easy to manipulate and control.

They Don't Like Criticism

When an individual escalates a situation at the slightest provocation, then you may be dealing with a malignant narcissist. If it is more common when there is criticism directed at the individual, then it is confirmed. Malignant narcissists don't do well with criticism.

They believe that they are always right, so there is a need to deflect any criticism that may expose them. To do this, they will quickly take an offensive stance when they receive criticism. This may be in the form of comments with the intent to belittle the individual voicing out their criticism.

They Engage in Psychological Projection

Projection explains a situation in which an individual performs an action but attributes these actions to another individual. It is an act that they perform to avoid admitting that they aren't perfect. Instead, they project these imperfections onto others.

A simple example is a situation in which a narcissist tells a lie and then turns around to call the person behind him a liar. This is the narcissist projecting his/her shortcomings on the other person.

The narcissist will continually accuse others of having this shortcoming without accepting that they are also culprits of the same action.

They Refuse to Admit to any Wrongdoing

For every action you take, there is always a consequence. Some of these consequences may be negative and will affect the lives of others. It is up to every individual to take responsibility for the consequences of their actions, no matter how difficult.

This simple explanation is something that malignant narcissists don't accept. In most situations, you can expect a narcissist to engage in denial when there is a need to take responsibility for any damage resulting from their actions.

If they do accept the action, they will look for ways to justify this action and appear as a victim. As a result of this justification, they will resort to blame-shifting to escape being held responsible for these actions.

They are Egocentric

With their inflated ego, some people do a good job making every conversation about them. These individuals don't have to be narcissists to be egocentric. Nonetheless, there is a crucial difference between both classes.

Egocentric individuals take steps to see things from the point of view of others. This will prompt them to reflect on their actions and the impact it has on other individuals.

For the egocentric narcissist, the story is quite different. Firstly, they want to be the center of attention while expecting compliments from others. Secondly, they try to manipulate a situation to align with their views and will get angry when people don't see things from their perspective.

Malignant narcissists often concern themselves with how people think about them, and due to their egocentric behavior, they may make wrong assumptions on how people view them.

They Need People to Pay Attention to Them

One of the reasons why a narcissist will try to appear attractive to you is for you to give them the attention they desire. This is you acting as the narcissistic supply. Narcissists often have lots of people they use to get this supply.

The attention a malignant narcissist craves includes both the negative and positive attention. Their aggression and the ease with which they can get into fights makes it easy to get this negative attention.

The reason why a malignant narcissist craves attention is to reinforce their self-esteem. To overcome their thoughts on how much others love them, they need this attention and adoration from others.

CHAPTER 6

The Covert Narcissist

In understanding the covert narcissist, it is essential that you first understand the use of covert and overt in psychology. These are two terms that psychologists use in explaining the behavior of an individual. Covert behaviors are those that are not easy to notice while overt behaviors refer to those that are easily identifiable.

In categorizing the various types of narcissists, the use of covert and overt behaviors is an essential factor. This difference in behavior is what separates the covert narcissist from other types of narcissists. In diagnosing a person with narcissistic personality disorder, the standards used are the same. The significant similarities that all kinds of narcissist share is the goal they intend to achieve.

The approach they take toward achieving this goal is different. They still retain the lack of empathy and sense of self-importance that is common with all narcissists.

The arrogance, loudness, and insensitivity of overt narcissists are clear signs that make it easy to single them out from a crowd. They can go as far as attracting both negative and positive attention to ensure that they remain in the spotlight.

They are usually the individuals doing the most in any room or gathering.

While you can classify the overt narcissists as extroverts, the covert narcissists fit right in with the introverts. A covert narcissist can get you trapped without you noticing anything different. With the overt narcissists, you see these behaviors from afar. This shows that the manipulative skill of the covert narcissist depends mainly on their ability to go unnoticed.

In a relationship with a covert narcissist, you only start to notice the signs of the narcissistic personality when you start experiencing low self-esteem due to love-starvation or emotional investment mismatch. This is often after investing a lot of time into the relationship.

What you must remember about the covert narcissist is that they don't fit into the general description of the narcissist. They are not the charming individual who is continuously taking actions to get others to stroke their ego in public. They are subtle and tend to be more discreet in their abuse.

They are indirect in their approach to everything. Like other narcissists, they feel they are superior, but won't outrightly tell you they are. The covert narcissist is perfect at subtly suggesting that they are better than you.

Although it is not direct like in the case of other narcissists, you still feel the same way afterward. To understand the covert narcissist better, there are some traits that you should know about.

Key Traits and Behaviors

In determining if an individual is a covert narcissist, there are certain traits and behaviors you must look out for. These are defined in this section. It is worth noting that while these traits define this form of narcissist, a covert narcissist may exhibit some and not all these traits.

They might show some of these traits sparingly, while others will be prominent throughout the time of the relationship. Spotting any of these signs regularly is an indication that you are dealing with a covert narcissist.

They are Extremely Sensitive Individuals

The first thing I would like you to understand is that an individual is not narcissistic just because they are extremely sensitive. It is common for people to take criticism pretty hard. What differentiates a covert narcissist from a highly sensitive individual is how they react to the criticism.

They take criticism personally and get offended and upset when anyone criticizes their views or actions. This can make it difficult to talk to a covert narcissist. You continuously have to carefully select your words to prevent them from having an abusive outburst.

Their sensitivity to criticism is noticeable in one of two ways. The covert narcissist can either show signs of withdrawal when there is criticism or take up a defensive stance and reinforce it with their smugness. This makes it easy for the covert narcissist to dismiss any form of constructive criticism.

When you injure the ego of a covert narcissist with your comments, they try to cover up how much the comments hurt them. They will choose to become detached rather than state the reason for the cold behavior.

They are Passive Aggressive

To punish you when you go against them, it is common for covert narcissists to implement passive-aggressive tactics. These tactics are in place to enable the narcissist to retain control and hurt you when necessary.

One of the most common ways through which the covert narcissist will display acts of passive-aggressiveness is offering to help without delivering on this help. This is just one action that the covert narcissist will take.

The passive-aggressive behaviors of the covert narcissist are often due to their sense of entitlement and will be put on display if you decide to say no to their demands. It doesn't matter how irrational you view these demands; they want them met. If you decide to stand up to the covert narcissist, then you are poking directly at their ego.

Their hostility is the defense mechanism that is in place to address such situations. If you want to understand the passive-aggressive behaviors of the narcissist fully, look out for the following actions they take to hurt others:

Blame Shifting

This is the inability of the covert narcissist to take responsibility for their actions. It always has to be the fault of someone else. If they fail at a task due to negligence or irresponsibility, they will have someone else take the fall.

Gaslighting is the preferred tactic of the covert narcissist. Using this tool, they will twist the truths of an event to create a scenario in which the blame lies on another individual. Using this simple technique, everyone forgets about the unruly behavior, professional misconduct, and failures of the narcissist. Their focus now rests on the victim of the gaslighting tactics.

If you have a narcissist in your life, getting to work late is due to your inability to wake them up at the right time. A night out drinking is their way to overcome the stress you are causing them in their opinion. These are some simple blame-shifting actions that you may assume to be normal–they are signs of a covert narcissist.

Hostility

Covert narcissists have their share of inadequacies and insecurities that they try to cover up. As a way of covering up these negative traits, they resort to tactics that offer a sense of superiority and self-assurance. They try to make people around them feel unhappy and miserable.

Hostility from the covert narcissist is usually in the form of verbal hostility. This action can either be an unconscious or conscious effort on the part of the narcissist. Your reaction to the hostility is also an excellent opportunity for the covert narcissist to receive his/her narcissistic supply.

There are different areas in which the narcissist can engage in verbal hostility. They can display this passive-aggressive behavior anytime you show interest in a new skill or develop a new hobby. They will talk down on your abilities while also criticizing any new idea you come up with during the relationship.

Sabotage

The covert narcissist performs his/her passive-aggressive actions subtly. There is often a disguise to ensure that these actions can sneak past your radar. This is how you get your punishment for any form of assertiveness that the narcissist misinterprets.

There are various ways that this can happen. They might interfere with you engaging in any activity that will yield positive growth in your life or disclose information that can hurt your reputation to others. Although it might seem unintentional, these are deliberate actions of the narcissist.

If you have a prior agreement with the narcissist, they can also choose to renege on this agreement. They will also engage in blame-shifting to make you take responsibility for these actions.

Humor

Narcissists engage in humor frequently. This may be to ridicule you and lure you into a humor trap. In their display of passive-aggressive behaviors, the covert narcissist will add a bit of hostility and sarcasm to the humor.

They don't take time to point out things that are bothering them. They don't intend to show any form of weakness. Instead, they will express their disapproval and anger through hostile humor. This is their way of telling you that they reject your actions.

The hostile humor is more effective when they apply it in public. They make hostile comments in a playful manner to others to laugh at you. This can make you feel stupid around your friends.

The use of passive-aggressiveness by the covert narcissist is essential in reestablishing their sense of entitlement and superiority, which they feel you have damaged due to your actions.

Smugness

Smugness defines the trait of an individual who shows extreme pride in their achievements or themselves. In the case of the covert narcissist, they exhibit this in a quiet manner. This is what differentiates them from the other narcissists that are more extroverted. It appears in the form of various non-verbal cues.

The smugness and feeling of superiority of the covert narcissist are noticeable in the way they sigh, roll their eyes, yawn, and have an inability to establish eye contact. If that isn't enough to identify them, then you can look out for the bored look on their face or the unenthusiastic vibe they give off while listening to you.

They are better at observing what others are doing in a judgmental manner while making gestures. In the way they speak, they are often judgmental with their remarks not only trying to assert their superiority but to also confuse and belittle you.

If they decide to offer any form of encouragement, it doesn't align with the negativity that their body language and actions usually give off.

In a conversation with a covert narcissist, you can notice their enthusiasm while they speak. While talking, every comment they make usually focuses on promoting their perspective on a matter. As soon as it is your turn to speak, they suddenly become uninterested in anything you have to say, and suddenly fall prey to the smallest distractions.

If you are lucky to get a covert narcissist who listens to what you say, you can be sure he/she is doing so to pick one or two comments that they can use in judging you later. The comments they make are often critical of your views with their main objective being to humiliate and belittle you for these opinions.

Like every narcissist with a mask, the smugness of the covert narcissist acts as their mask. Covert narcissists are insecure and vulnerable. Afraid of being exposed, they resort to this smugness to cover up who they indeed are. Understanding this will help in minimizing the effect of the hurtful remarks from the covert narcissist.

They Don't Show Empathy

Most of the behaviors and characteristics of the covert narcissist make them stand out from the other types of narcissists. One of the few traits that they all have in common is the lack of empathy. It is typical for a covert narcissist to ignore your feelings.

The lack of empathy hurts. If you are unlucky enough to get into an accident while driving the car of a covert narcissist, you can expect them to worry more about their vehicle than your condition.

Their response when you call them out on this behavior will often focus on how they are on the losing end of the event.

An Unusual Feeling of Self-Importance

The feeling of self-importance is noticeable in the attempts by the covert narcissist to appear special. They will bring up the silly excuse of being unique, which makes it difficult for them to connect with others.

They make superficial comments to establish and reassure themselves of their self-importance. While it may be in a bid to mask their vulnerabilities, the covert narcissist can get on your nerves with these comments. They claim that they are victims of constant misinterpretation and isolation.

They form Detached Relationships

Unlike other individuals who try to connect with people, the covert narcissist doesn't go to this extent to create relationships. They are comfortable with a conceited view. In this view, you are simply an object that they will manipulate to their heart's content.

Beneath their mask, narcissists lack most of the skills necessary for excellent communication. These inadequacies are what they try to cover up using this defense mechanism. This will ensure that the narcissist can set a barrier to prevent anyone from encroaching into their safe space.

Due to this inability to develop meaningful relationships, the covert narcissist searches for other ways to fill this void. They can do this by engaging in activities that don't depend on the influence of other humans. Activities that fall into this classification include hobbies such as watching movies, reading, and playing video games. Devoting most of their time to their work is another way they occupy their time.

You may have a covert narcissist in your life who has a few friends around. You should take note of how he/she treats these friends. They are known to cut off communication with ease.

The bond of their friendship is shallow and doesn't run deep like other forms of friendship. All these are steps to protect the narcissist. If they let anyone get too close, they run the risk of revealing their true self.

The Four Types of Narcissism

They are Self-Absorbed

The self-absorption of the covert narcissist is noticeable in their need for every discussion to be about them. If you engage them in any form of conversation that doesn't include any topic that is about them, they show a lack of interest in the conversation.

Self-absorption is what differentiates a covert narcissist from someone you will consider shy or introverted. An introvert is usually a quiet person who can be an excellent listener. In the case of the covert narcissist, they lack the qualities of a great listener.

Due to their poor listening skills, they are quick to draw the wrong conclusions in a situation or about someone else. In any given situation, you will often take time to assess your behavior and actions to determine if they are appropriate. This is what you consider self-awareness.

Covert narcissists lack this self-awareness. This is why they are unable to identify their self-absorption. In some cases, it is merely the narcissist being unwilling to accept this fault.

Their focus in every situation is always on themselves. Therefore, they are only looking for how to benefit from a situation. This includes having their needs and wants to be met regardless of how selfish it will appear to others.

CHAPTER 7

The Communal Narcissist

Just like the other types, the communal narcissist is proof that you can find narcissism being portrayed in unique manners. One of the signs of a communal narcissist is their approach. Unlike other types, communal narcissists use communal means in achieving their goals.

These communal means are actions that people consider as prosocial behaviors. They can include listening to others, achieving a common goal with others, or making a commitment to others. These actions make them very much unlike the narcissists who are supposed to be self-centered individuals.

Explicit and Implicit Views in Communal Narcissism

The truth about the communal narcissist is that while they believe that they possess these prosocial behaviors, people who interact with them state otherwise. How is this possible? Are the communal narcissists altering their reality to think that they possess these communal traits? An easy way to understand this is through explicit and implicit views.

An explicit self-view refers to the actions you take to assess the various traits that make you stand out from a group in an intentional manner. The belief that you can run faster than an individual standing beside you is a form of explicit self-view.

The implicit self-views refer to these self-assessment actions when they are performed subconsciously. They offer a more accurate reflection of what you can provide since the subconscious manner in which they are done doesn't give room for the influence of your need for self-presentation. Using the same example from earlier, the implicit self-view can be observed if you are having doubts about how fast you can run.

Using these definitions of implicit and explicit self-views, we can better define what is going on with the communal narcissists. In their explicit self-views, the communal narcissist intentionally adopts the notion that they commit to helping others. For the implicit self-views, they don't feel helpful to others.

You can consider the communal claims of this form of narcissist as a form of hypocrisy and lip-service to make themselves look good. Communal narcissists often play considerable roles in communities while being destructive in their homes. This means you can find them volunteering for community projects or taking the spotlight in charitable actions.

These actions make it difficult for anyone to believe that such individuals are narcissists. It is only noticeable to their close circle of family and friends. Their relationship with this circle can be described as being devoid of any form of love.

The Communal Narcissism Inventory

Identifying the various forms of narcissists often depends on you looking into their key traits and behaviors. The same also applies to the communal narcissist, but there is another way to do this. It is through the application of the Communal Narcissism Inventory.

This inventory functions by asking a person to rate themselves from 1 to 7 for a set of statements. On this scale, one signifies that you strongly disagree while seven means that you strongly agree. There are 16 statements you will find in the inventory (Streep, 2016):

- I am excellent at listening to others.
- My actions in the future will usher in world peace and justice.

- Having me as a friend is the best you can imagine.
- I am more understanding than any other person.
- As a parent, I am going to be the best in the world.
- Finding solutions to various world problems will earn me my fame.
- No one I know is as helpful as I am.
- My impact on the lives of others is enriching.
- I will bring freedom to the people.
- I will create a solution to alleviate poverty around the world.
- My influence on others in a positive.
- My good deeds will earn me recognition.
- I will work towards creating a world more beautiful than this.
- I am an extremely trustworthy individual.
- Enhancing the well-being of others is one of the reasons why I will be famous.
- In my environment, I offer the most care.

Narcissists that strongly agree with these statements are usually communal narcissists. These statements are all indications of traits of communalism. Remember, the communal narcissists still retain their predisposition of self-preservation. Their ability to empathize with others is nonexistent and they possess the other characteristics of narcissists.

This often means that their acts of communalism are to derive self-validation.

Key Traits and Behaviors

They Get Their Supply from Engaging in Communal Work

Communal narcissists are like other narcissists since they also want people to stroke their ego. To achieve this, the first step they take is engaging in communal work. These actions make them look helpful to others. The reason for this action is what separates a communal narcissist from regular people.

As an individual, it is common to want to help others. Doing good deeds is often a way to render your service to humanity. Your goal of providing these services is because you have an inner drive to do so.

For the communal narcissists, they do these good deeds to have people stroke their ego. This is one of the fundamental wants that drives a narcissist. Unlike other people that want to help others, the communal narcissist will announce these good deeds to the world.

This is to get people to reply by telling them how amazing they are as humans. This is how they get their narcissistic supply.

They are Constantly Talking about how Helpful They are to Others

The communal narcissist is the kind of narcissist that always wants people to know how helpful they are to other people. You will find them continuously pointing out the prosocial traits that make them look good to others. They will say things like:

- Look how empathic I am
- I am such a great listener
- I was very helpful to my friend during his trying times

All these are actions that point them out as being helpful to others in situations when it matters the most.

If they do get the opportunity to do the right thing, this is an excellent way for them to show off their helpfulness to others. By doing this, they get others to gather around them to hear more about how helpful they have been.

They Consider Themselves as Givers and Not Takers

Taking in this sense doesn't necessarily translate to collecting stuff from other people. As a giver, the communal narcissist believes they offer more value to others. Here are some of the thoughts that make people out as givers:

- How much they cooperate with others
- How much they can be trusted
- How helpful they are to others

Their Private Life Differs from their Public

Being helpful in the community is an excellent way to stand out in the public eye. It is a unique way of leaving a lasting impression on other individuals. Continually engaging in communal work is one of the means through which communal narcissists maintain their reputation.

In private, when they are with their family or friends, they can be very destructive. This might involve being a prominent member of the local church while constantly denigrating and putting down family members.

CHAPTER 8

Understanding What Obstacles You Need to Overcome

Obstacles in your life are in place to prevent you from making progress. In making progress toward healing from narcissistic abuse, there are certain obstacles you must overcome. These obstacles are like mental barriers set up by the narcissist.

As a step toward recovery, overcoming these barriers will also help in starting a new relationship if the narcissist in your life happens to be a partner you must leave. Some of the obstacles you must overcome are as follows:

Lack of Boundaries

The best target for a narcissist is an individual that doesn't set boundaries. These individuals are easily identifiable by their compulsion to please others. This is a habit they develop to get the attention they crave.

If you always say yes to every request you get, then you lack boundaries. It also gives the narcissist the impression that they can easily project their beliefs and needs onto you. They know that to avoid any form of conflict, you will be willing to go the extra mile to please them.

There are various reasons why you may have a lack of boundaries. The first may be due to your training while growing up. This is true for individuals with a childhood in an abusive home.

Such children grow up to see the world differently. In their case, they often grow up believing that there is always a punishment for defying anyone in authority. To avoid such punishment, they develop a people-pleasing habit.

A lack of boundaries when you have a narcissist in your life means that you won't be able to identify when things are wrong. You may also have boundaries that are impressionable. This is due to your empathy, and this makes it easy to fall for the manipulation of the narcissist.

Looking at it from the perspective of the narcissist, they also lack boundaries. What this means is that they don't see anything wrong when they decide to ignore the boundaries you put up. It is more challenging to deal with them when you take proper steps, and it seems ineffective.

To overcome this obstacle, you must be ready to add consequences for every action they take and implement them. This is one effective way to deter them.

Psychological Trap

The psychological trap that you fall into during your time with a narcissist is an obstacle that you must overcome if you want to escape the narcissist. This trap is noticeable in the form of the co-dependency that you develop during your relationship with the narcissist. There are various destructive side effects of this trap that you must understand.

Being co-dependent implies that you have gotten to a point at which you have very low self-esteem. This is an effect of your dysfunctional relationship with the narcissist. Getting out of this trap is totally up to you since lack of empathy in a narcissist negates all feelings of wrongdoing.

Breaking free of the psychological trap of the narcissist is not a simple feat. For some individuals, getting out of this trap means reaching a breaking point. This is a point at which you suddenly start questioning everything around you and realize that the narcissist offers no value.

The Four Types of Narcissism

One step you can take in overcoming the psychological trap includes getting help from a professional.

Starvation for Love

Love is unattainable with a narcissistic partner. When you think of starvation, you understand it to imply a situation in which you are unable to find anything to eat. Due to this lack of food, you lose focus on everything else and focus on finding something to quench your hunger.

The same scenario also applies when you are starved for love. You can describe this as a situation in which you have a constant deprivation of affection or love for so long, it makes it the only thing you crave. This is common with victims of the narcissist.

If you are unable to overcome it, this starvation of love can expose you to narcissistic abuse in the future. In your quest to find someone to love you, it makes you an easy target through love-bombing. You instantly fall for anyone willing to shower you with compliments that evoke the feeling of being loved that you crave so much.

When you stay in a narcissistic relationship for so long, you forget what love truly means. This means you might end up going from one bad relationship to another. Depending on how forceful you are in your search for love, it is common to cause the right individuals to distance themselves.

There are times you will find yourself in a relationship without a commitment from your partner. In such cases, starvation of love can make you ignore these signs. Rather than face reality, you will fantasize about the time your partner will start showing empathy as you change certain behaviors.

Overcoming the starvation of love usually requires you to heal on your own. This means that you avoid relationships for the duration of the healing process. While some individuals are lucky to meet a person that genuinely shows them love, you may not be so fortunate.

You must develop a means through which you can become independent. This is possible through self-love. By learning to appreciate yourself, you can lessen the effects of starvation of love. As you begin to adopt the self-love idea, you can get back on the market to search for a partner.

Being independent helps you in standing firm when choosing your partner. If you see any red flag, you quickly shut down communication before it goes too far.

Low Shame Tolerance and Low Self Esteem

Low self-esteem is a massive obstacle that you must overcome in your quest. The main reason why you find it difficult to cut ties with a narcissist is due to low self-esteem. Rather than making healthy decisions, you accept to remain in an abusive relationship.

The feelings of self-doubt and worthlessness that come with low self-esteem can make you choose an abusive relationship over being lonely. Overcoming this low self-esteem requires a change in your beliefs. Instead of adopting negativity, there is a need to believe in yourself.

There is also the problem of low shame tolerance. Interacting with a narcissist means you are continually going to experience ridicule. A low shame tolerance can hurt you in such situations.

You must develop yourself mentally if you want to withstand the actions of the narcissist. Low shame tolerance will get you feeling down and worthless every time the narcissist attacks you.

Fear and Guilt

The human mind is a complex entity, and this shows in how we think. In a narcissistic relationship, it is common for individuals to go through various unhealthy challenges. These include low self-esteem, guilt, emotional mismatch, shame, and so on.

Regardless of these issues with the narcissist, some individuals still choose to stay in the relationship. There are various reasons why an individual may decide to stay, and this includes financial stability, religion, children, and culture. These are valid reasons why it may be necessary to stay with the narcissist

In other narcissistic relationships, the victim of the abuse may decide to remain due to their fear. There are two ways through which fear can be an issue. It can show up as the fear of being alone or the fear of missing out.

It is common for victims of narcissistic abuse to stick around due to their fear of being alone. They understand that they are in an abusive relationship, but pick this option over being alone. Due to their low self-esteem, they don't see the possibility of getting into another relationship soon.

The Four Types of Narcissism

I use the fear of missing out to describe a situation in which the victim holds on to the relationship, thinking that the narcissist will change. This means that the narcissist will improve on his/her behaviors and start showing signs of a good partner. They want to be at the side of the narcissist when this change occurs.

In truth, a narcissist can't change their personality. A victim that grasps this truth will find it easy to let go. To get over the fear of being alone, learning to pick the lessons from different life experiences help.

Enhancing your self-esteem can help you understand your worth. If you know your worth, then you can conclude that there are others out there that will also see this worth. These individuals will accept and adore you for who you are.

Guilt offers positive benefits to an individual depending on how they approach it. Some individuals examine themselves and engage in activities to improve their personality through their guilt. Other individuals, such as co-dependents, experience a form of unhealthy guilt.

Classifying guilt as either healthy or unhealthy is a simple way to differentiate it. Healthy guilt promotes empathy and encourages actions that cause a person to change. On the other hand, individuals who experience unhealthy guilt assume themselves to be inadequate and inferior to others.

Unhealthy guilt is one of the results of a lack of boundaries and shame. This form of guilt hurts the self-esteem of an individual. If you want to have excellent self-esteem, self-acceptance and self-forgiveness are essential.

When working toward a goal, getting into a new relationship, or doing things that make you happy, unhealthy guilt can damage your efforts. The condemnation that comes with this form of guilt may be conscious or unconscious.

If you are unable to control your guilt, it is common to keep punishing yourself for everything that happened during your relationship with the narcissist. This can continue after escaping the toxic relationship. The first step to overcoming unhealthy guilt is to learn how to forgive.

Forgive yourself for everything. There are times when other people make mistakes that affect you directly. In these cases, do you hold this single mistake against them for life? In the same manner you move on and forgive this mistake, you also have to forgive yourself.

The next step to overcoming unhealthy guilt is to know your boundaries. If you fail to put up a boundary, your guilt may stem from the behavior of the narcissist. It is noticeable in your willingness to accept the blame for their irrational actions.

Another common reason for unhealthy guilt is due to the projection by your abuser. Accepting the projections by the narcissist will often lead to unhealthy guilt. Creating ironclad boundaries could help in limiting projections by the narcissist.

In overcoming guilt, you must understand that pretending to be affected by ignorance doesn't make it go away. This is only a temporary reprieve. To eliminate your guilt, the steps you must take include acceptance and self-examination. This will help in determining the right actions to take going forward.

Lacking a Sense of Shame

As a human, shame is a feeling that often results in pain. Various thoughts evoke shame, including humiliation and thinking that we aren't good enough. In the case of some children, they start experiencing shame when they undergo humiliation by their parents regularly.

One of the problems that shame causes is interference. It interferes with your ability to have any experience that you can deem favorable. These are experiences that cause you to feel hope, joy, or humor.

In contending with a narcissist, you have to also contend with their lacking sense of shame. Yes, narcissists are shameless individuals. Regular acts of humiliation that will get you down for a whole week does not affect them. Narcissists overcome shame due to their lack of guilt.

Once they have their sights on a goal, there is little you can do to stop them. They have a strong will that they use in reinforcing their sense of superiority and entitlement. Their lack of empathy also plays a role in this shamelessness.

This is something you must overcome in dealing with them because they have no moral line in their dealings. They have no issues lying to others about your actions.

Shamelessness means they don't experience any mental or emotional repercussions for their actions. They don't feel bad when they leave you deep in debt or damage you psychologically.

CHAPTER 9

Create an Indestructible Support Structure and Restore Your Self-Esteem

Support structures are an essential piece of solving the puzzle to your recovery. In medicine, doctors understand that a corrective surgery isn't enough to heal a patient. They also require emotional support.

Since the doctor can't provide this emotional support, they advise you to stay with friends, family, or join support groups that can accelerate the recovery. The same also applies when recovering from narcissistic abuse. You need to find a structure that will offer the emotional support you require.

There are different ways to create a support structure. Any of these options can offer the support you require. To make it indestructible, it is vital you implement each option. They include the following options:

Find Allies and Friends

Friends and allies can help you during your time recovering from narcissistic abuse. You must find only real friends and allies to ensure you get the right support. Not everyone around you is a true friend.

How the Narcissist gets your friends

The smear campaign of the narcissist often makes it easy to identify those people around you who can form your allies and those that are real friends. Loyalty is one of the critical traits of a true friend. The smear campaign will test the loyalty of those you call your friends.

Some friends will believe the lies of the narcissist without questioning it. You can group them into either toxic or naïve friends. Those friends that you classify as toxic refers to those who weren't out for your well-being from the onset.

These are individuals who have something to gain from the narcissist—favors, flattery, or status. Therefore, they will choose to follow the narcissist for these gains. It will be futile to try to approach these individuals with the truth—they have no interest in it.

On the other hand, those who are naïve refer to the friends that cave in the face of intimidation. They don't try to escape or fight the situation; they accept things as they come. They will choose to believe the more powerful force—the narcissist.

There is a separate group of friends that you refer to as real friends. These are the individuals who don't accept the lies from the narcissist and his/her allies. Your real friends will take your side and do their best to protect your reputation and mental health when dealing with narcissistic abuse.

You must understand that in escaping and overcoming narcissistic abuse, you might lose some of your friends along the line. When you decide it is time to move on from a narcissistic relationship, you can expect them to put up a fight. This involves playing the victim to get mutual friends on their side.

Getting Past Isolation

When recovering from narcissistic abuse, it is more common to find out that you have lost a lot of friendships. One of the critical moves of a narcissist is getting you to steer clear of your friends. The effect of this isolation becomes more noticeable after escaping the narcissistic relationship.

You suddenly notice most of your friends have moved on with their lives during the period the narcissist isolated you. Having people to talk to is helpful when recovering from narcissistic abuse. The options available to you include making new friends or trying to rekindle old friendships.

Rekindling old friendships can be easy if you take the right steps. The first action you must take is to contact these old friends. Let them know the reason for the breakdown in communication.

You can also take a trip so you can meet these friends in person. If they send you an invite and you agree to honor the invite, make sure you show up. It is crucial you understand that things may not be the same as the past–adapt to these changes.

There is also the option of making new friends. This is possible if you decide to volunteer for a project in your community. A support group can also offer the perfect opportunity to meet individuals that understand you.

The internet also offers excellent opportunities to interact with other individuals through discussions on social platforms. Make the most of this opportunity. In overcoming and recovering from narcissistic abuse, doing it alone isn't the best option. Have friends and allies around that can offer physical, mental, and emotional support.

Prepare yourself for rejection when trying to make new friends or rekindle old friendships. Remember, a friendship depends on the two parties for success. You must also put in the effort to make sure your friends also benefit from the interaction in one way or another. Try to be a good listener.

Find Support Groups and Talk to People Who Are Going Through the Same Thing

Protecting yourself from narcissistic abuse and recovering afterward can be difficult if you don't know how to go about it. One of the excellent options that help in both situations is to join a support group.

A support group refers to a group of people who share a similar problem that strengthens the bond between them. Due to this problem, each member of the group usually experiences some similar situations in life. Through these experiences, it is easier for others to overcome some challenges.

A simple example is a support group for individuals trying to overcome alcohol addiction. In this group, there will be specific individuals who have overcome their addiction while others are taking steps to do so. Individuals who have overcome addiction can help by offering some coping strategies, information on what to expect during the process, and more.

In other cases, a support group can help in offering the essential emotional support that you need to overcome certain challenges. Since they have gone through or are currently experiencing the same difficulty, it is simpler for them to understand how you are feeling. This is often much more effective than relying on your friends or parents.

Why should you join a support group?

In addition to meeting people with a similar challenge as yours, there are other reasons why you should join a support group. In a relationship with a narcissist or overcoming narcissistic abuse, these can include the following:

- Understanding the narcissist better
- Learning how to set healthy boundaries that work
- Getting feedback on real-time applications of certain strategies
- Talking about your feelings in an honest manner
- To eliminate the sense of isolation and loneliness
- To gain the necessary motivation to keep pushing

How do you choose the right support group?

Just because a support group focuses on narcissistic abuse doesn't mean it is the right one for you. There are a few questions you must ask. The answers to this question can help you identify a support group that will guide you on the right path towards overcoming narcissistic abuse.

Here are some of the questions to ask:

- Does the group have a facilitator or moderator?
- Did this individual go through any formal training?
- Is there a duration for each meeting?
- What is the focus of this support group?
- Do I have to pay to be a part of the group?
- How does the group handle confidentiality?
- How frequently do meetings hold, and where is the location of the meeting?

If you identify any other question that can help you in making the right decision, be sure to ask. Your questions are your tools in ensuring you find a support group that doesn't worsen your situation.

Are there signs that can act as red flags when selecting a support group?

Most support groups do their best in solving the problems of the members. Regardless, some simple signs are clear indications of a support group that won't be very helpful to you. These signs include:

- Requesting an exorbitant amount to grant entry into the group
- Trying to get members to pay for services or products

You must understand that some support groups require a fee. This fee shouldn't be too high that it feels like extortion to the members. Also, advertising a product or service once or twice isn't harmful, but if the moderator repeatedly tries to pressurize members into making a purchase, it should be clear that the group is more focused on profits.

Choosing an online support group over one that requires a physical presence

The internet makes things a lot easier for individuals going through narcissistic abuse. If you don't like the idea of meeting up with other individuals of a support group in person, you can interact with these individuals online. You must understand that while these may offer some benefits, there are specific issues you need to prepare yourself to overcome.

Some of the advantages of the online support group are as follows:

- The option to remain anonymous to protect your privacy
- Opportunity to participate in the group without a time restraint
- It offers a more comfortable option for individuals that have a tight schedule
- An alternative for individuals who lack support group meetup close to their location

With these few benefits, certain demerits often make a face-to-face meetup more appealing to individuals. Here are some of the downsides of the online support group:

- It limits the time you spend with those that are physically present to offer support
- It is easy to misinterpret a message from other group participants if the sentences aren't correctly structured

- Due to a large community of users, there is often excess information as well as some misinformation
- You can expect some unruly behavior and unnecessary comments from members who take advantage of the option to remain anonymous

While online support groups offer some excellent benefits over a face-to-face support group, you can have a hard time adjusting to some of its unique aspects. You must weigh the pros and cons when deciding if this will be the best option for you. The next step is identifying a support group that works for you.

Getting Information on Helpful Support Groups

There are lots of support groups available to help individuals in different locations around the world. Finding a group that will meet your needs will require a bit of research. Here are some options that you can utilize in finding such groups:

National Institutes of Health Websites

These sites often have information on support groups that can be helpful against various challenges. These challenges include health conditions and diseases, as well as other issues like alcohol addiction and narcissistic abuse.

Restore Self-Esteem

Your self-esteem refers to how you see yourself. It is a form of self-evaluation that enables you to determine your worth. It includes your ability to identify and accept your strengths and weaknesses as an individual.

Having good self-esteem allows you to express kindness to yourself, believe in yourself, assert your decisions, and take on new challenges. Self-esteem is also essential in moving on from mistakes in the past without placing the blame on yourself. This is a crucial aspect you need to hold on to when overcoming narcissistic abuse.

One of the damaging effects of narcissistic abuse is the lower self-esteem of victims. The various actions a narcissist takes are focused on diminishing the self-esteem of their victim. Gaslighting, smear campaigns, triangulation, devaluation, and discard all have this in common.

To restore your self-esteem means to take control of your life once again. It is freeing yourself from the psychological barriers that the narcissist has put in place to make you willing to dive back into the relationship if they come calling.

The first step in restoring your self-esteem is to force yourself to take responsibility. Inability to accept responsibility for some of the outcomes of the narcissistic relationship is a significant reason why some individuals are unable to restore their self-esteem. Accepting responsibility is more difficult in practice.

This difficulty stems from the similarity blame-shifting shares with taking responsibility. When you decide to accept responsibility, you are choosing to blame yourself for how long you allowed the abuse to continue. This can be painful to accept.

To fully understand why you are responsible, there are specific questions you must answer. These include the following:

- Why did you decide to change who you are to please someone else?
- Why did you overlook the red flags anytime they popped up?
- Why did you stay in the relationship despite your inability to speak on your feelings?
- Why do you think you are unworthy of being wanted or loved again?

By answering these questions, you will notice several things. The first is that during the narcissistic abuse, you were also an enabler. Another thing you notice is that you need to work on and improve yourself to avoid being an enabler in the future.

Taking responsibility is a choice you must make on your own. It is through this choice that you can accept areas that need growth and self-improvement. Once you start taking responsibility, the next step is to engage in self-care.

Self-care refers to the act of putting yourself first in most situations. One part of self-care involves showing yourself love. During your relationship with the narcissist, the starvation of love is often the reason for your diminishing self-esteem.

The actions you take are often in a bid to get the narcissist to show love and other emotions. In truth, you are merely trying to change their personality. You are working on their problems while ignoring your problems.

An overhaul of your beliefs is necessary for supporting your decision to engage in self-care. When growing up, the social norms we come to accept include thinking of others and helping them before tending to personal needs. These norms don't apply to healthy self-care.

Healthy self-care involves taking care of your needs before the needs of others. To do this, you must rediscover yourself. Since you are freeing yourself from the needs of the narcissist, it also implies that you are changing the things you do daily.

It's no longer a race to meet the needs and do what the narcissist requires of you. There is a high possibility that you have no idea what makes you happy any longer. It is time to observe your life and ask yourself the following questions:

- Do you prefer being outdoors?
- Do you have a preference when it comes to movies and music?
- Are there certain hobbies that you love engaging in?
- How would you rather spend your free time?

These are some simple questions that can help you understand your needs and wants. Self-care must be a priority if you're going to improve your self-esteem.

If you take an old car for a paint job, you notice that it becomes more valuable than it was without the paint job. This is what happens when you start experiencing a sudden change in appearance due to self-care. Your value steadily increases.

The time and effort you invest in yourself is proof of your worth. Continuous self-care means that your value will keep appreciating. It also means that you will become more protective.

This is what you can refer to as self-love. You no longer see yourself as a failure or insecure. Now you are so much more. Through self-love, it becomes easier to put up healthy boundaries.

With the knowledge of your self-worth, you can also learn to make the right choices. The reason for all these steps in raising your self-esteem is to gain better control over your life. Better control means you can prevent abuse from the narcissist.

If you are currently having no contact with a narcissist, you might wonder, "why will I ever go back to a narcissist?" The truth is that there is no way to prevent yourself from appealing to a narcissist. You can only control what you give the narcissist. When you understand your worth, you know that you must protect yourself as soon as you see the red flags.

CHAPTER 10

Breaking Out of an Unbreakable Trap

As humans, it is common for us to constantly be on the lookout for someone that you can spend time with. This is why humans are usually referred to as social beings. Our survival is dependent on interaction and cooperation between other humans.

This is one of the reasons why we seek out relationships. It is necessary to eliminate the feeling of isolation and emptiness that is common when you are alone. Our priority is to seek out the right person to form this relationship.

The right person often attracts you with their charm and charisma before you can get to know them better. The narcissist is aware of this and puts on a facade that makes him/her appear like the right person.

In a relationship with a non-narcissist, each individual does their best to match the efforts of the other. This doesn't apply in a relationship with the narcissist. The narcissist wants you to do all the work in the relationship.

Despite this, they will still take up the role of the victim when the relationship fails.

Creating a balance that is necessary for a relationship to work requires practice. No one is born perfect, so you have to improve the essential skill continually. In a relationship with a non-narcissist, developing this skill is possible.

In a relationship with a narcissist, there are certain traps the narcissist uses in getting you to lose a sense of this balance. This may involve the narcissist getting you to help them get through their challenges while they don't reciprocate this gesture when you find yourself in a problem.

In this chapter, you will learn about some of the traps that the narcissist uses and how to break free. Getting your freedom is essential in building a better life after your time with a narcissist.

Emotional Investment Mismatch and Trap

The emotional investment mismatch is a situation that occurs if the narcissist is unwilling to reciprocate any of the emotions you show. In most of the traps the narcissist use, they work on your lack of awareness. When you are conscious of their actions, it is easy to notice these minor details.

To understand why there is an emotional investment mismatch in a relationship with a narcissist, it is crucial you know the false self and true self of the narcissist discussed in an earlier. For a narcissist to match your emotional investment, you must show an emotion that they can mirror. As a non-narcissist, the emotions you display are those that make you vulnerable.

These are the emotions that the narcissist has locked away along with the true self. Since the narcissist is wearing the false self as a mask, they can't mirror these emotions. It will be a sign of vulnerability which the narcissist doesn't ever want to show to the world.

Another relevant term in understanding the emotional investment mismatch is the "limbic resonance." Limbic resonance is essential for creating a social connection with other individuals. It explains your ability to pick up the emotions of an individual you are interacting with through the limbic system.

The limbic system then makes it possible to adjust your emotional state to match that of the other individual. By achieving this limbic resonance, you understand that you have formed a connection with the other individual.

In the case of an interaction with a narcissist, this connection isn't formed. In a bid to create this connection, you increase the intensity of your emotions with the hopes that the narcissist will finally notice and match your emotions.

While this may seem inconsequential in your relationship with a narcissist, there is a side effect of increasing your emotional intensity regularly. Due to your experience with the narcissist, your view on connecting with other individuals will change. You conclude that you have to be forceful in your interactions or no one will listen to you.

In such interactions, you will go in with a high emotional intensity that is difficult to match by the other individual. This approach will make you project your emotions on the other person.

The emotional investment focuses on the emotion you impress on a person during an interaction. If you are telling someone the story of how you lost money to a bad investment, you can either end the conversation being shameful or being understood. If there is a sign of empathy in the other individual, then you know that they have matched your emotional investment level.

Understanding the Emotional Investment Trap

Now you know what emotional investment is all about. So, what does the emotional investment trap look like? This is a trap through which the narcissist flourishes.

What this trap offers them is a continuous flow of the narcissistic supply. The various emotions you show the narcissist are what fuel the narcissistic supply. This is why the emotional investment trap is in place.

The trap will have you increasing your emotional intensity in a bid to get the attention of the narcissist. When you try it the first time without positive results, it can be saddening, but you have a goal of connecting with the narcissist. To achieve this goal, you keep raising the intensity level.

In reality, you are already in a loop within the emotional investment trap. Due to the lack of empathy on the part of the narcissist, you also experience love-starvation. The result of the emotional investment trap is an individual with low self-esteem.

Breaking out of this trap may seem straightforward–but it isn't. It is common for victims to finally reach a point at which they no longer have an interest in investing in the narcissist. To keep you in the trap, the narcissist will go as far as showing signs of empathy and love.

Finally!– You make the wrong assumption that you have connected with the narcissist. In truth, these actions are all fake and is a plot by the narcissist to give you a glimmer of hope that there is the possibility of attaining the emotional balance that you desire.

If the display of empathy does not affect you, they will resort to using other tactics that will prompt engagement. All they need is the slightest reaction from you. Once this happens, you return to being the source of narcissistic supply.

Humor Trap

Humor is another powerful tool that narcissists can use to create a trap without you realizing what is happening. As a tool, narcissists can make use of humor in controlling and conditioning you to act in specific ways. The application of the humor trap is often in a gathering of friends to get you to go along with their plan.

You've probably heard someone say laughter is contagious. The narcissist does his/her best to make this your reality. Since you don't have narcissistic tendencies, your brain makes you understand that it is right to laugh along when someone else is laughing.

The narcissist uses this to their advantage. They laugh when they make simple comments and get you to do the same. If you conclude that this laughter is one of the personal tics of the narcissist, then you will be making a mistake.

Your laughter isn't dependent on your thoughts of the comments. You are laughing as a polite response and not because you find the comment amusing. The narcissist will slowly move on to sneaking mockery into these comments.

They will do this around others to make it difficult for you to call them out on this behavior. You try to take the joke since they also make these comments in a jovial manner. Repeating this action over time is a method of conditioning you.

The effect of this conditioning is the ease with which you laugh when the narcissist ridicules you both in public and private. This is an unhealthy acceptance you develop.

Conversation Trap

Narcissists use the conversation to get your attention so that they can talk about themselves. Unlike a regular discussion in which all participants share the spotlight equally, the narcissist finds a way to be the only one in the spotlight for the entire duration of the conversation. To do this, they will first take appropriate steps to ensure that you are invested in the conversation. To assure them of this investment, they will play nice by asking about your day or work. Since it is about you, there is a lot of investment into the conversation.

It is at this point that the narcissist will redirect the focus back to themselves. Unlike the narcissist, you understand how rude it is to interrupt others when they are talking. This is why you let them speak continuously on things that mean nothing to you. At the end of the conversation, all you gain is pent up frustration.

Refuse to Take the Bait

To break out of these traps that the narcissist will use, you must learn to identify when they are trying to bait you into the trap. If you can locate the bait, then you can avoid the hook. In this section, you will learn to avoid each of the traps discussed above.

Dodging the Emotional Investment Trap

To identify the bait for the emotional investment trap, you must first know what a relationship with an emotional match looks like. This is a relationship in which it is possible to establish a connection. Some of the characteristics of such relationships include:

- Two individuals that try to attain emotional resonance by matching their emotional intensity during the conversation
- A speaker that allows the listener to understand their message by simplifying it
- A speaker that gives room for their listener to ask questions or offer their perspective so that there can be a better understanding of the intention of the speaker
- A listener that isn't always trying to cut short the speaker

If you notice that interactions with the narcissist lacks any of these characteristics, then you should understand that they are trying to bait you into the emotional investment trap. The most straightforward sign of this trap is the inability to mirror your emotions.

When they are constantly trying to take over a conversation, you should know what is on their mind. You should end such conversations swiftly. If an individual doesn't understand, listen, or empathize with you, then it is an indication that you are getting into the emotional investment trap. Break free before you go in too deep.

Shutting Down the Humor Trap

The humor trap isn't funny. Let them know how you feel. Don't keep laughing when you know it isn't amusing to you.

Some successful relationships thrive on banter. This sort of banter involves everyone in the relationship participating. This is unlike in the case of the narcissist.

The narcissist will make sure you are always on the receiving end. They are always mocking you to feel good about themselves. The comments that the narcissists make when trying to get you into the humor trap often sound demeaning.

If you notice this, then you can let them know that you don't like it. Don't laugh when they do. Narcissists want to be in control, and this is your way of taking that away from them.

Escaping the Conversation Trap

The conversation trap is easy to notice. You can quickly identify when a person wants to talk about their endeavors throughout a conversation. If they act like you are nonexistent during the conversation, then it is a sign of the conversation trap.

If they hijack the conversation once you start talking about yourself, then know that they were only trying to get you into the conversation trap. You should end the conversation quickly.

If you try to sit through the conversation, you might end up in a mentally exhausting situation.

CHAPTER 11

Creating Ironclad Boundaries That Will Last

In your relationship with a narcissist, you will be wrong if you think you can get them to change with time. This train of thought is what exposes you to the narcissistic abuse. It is often best to stay away from a narcissistic individual.

Knowing all this, there are times when you can't stay away from them and can only find ways to deal with them. These situations include relationships with a narcissistic partner or parent, colleague, or after a relationship with a narcissistic partner with whom you have a child.

If left to run amok, a narcissist can ruin your life. This includes both your current relationship and any relationship you will have in the future. Why give them this much control over your future?

To prevent a narcissist from controlling how your life plays out, you must create firm boundaries to keep them out. The more effective the boundary you set with the narcissist, the minimal effects of the narcissistic abuse if it still occurs.

In a relationship, some people argue that there is no need for boundaries since it is expected that your partner should have an idea of the limits to the things you can take. This doesn't apply in the case of the narcissist. A clearly defined boundary is the only way to maintain a relationship with a narcissistic partner.

Boundaries in a relationship with a narcissist are essential if you want to develop and maintain your positive self-esteem. Boundaries encompass the values and beliefs that define who you are. These are the things you want your partner to respect in the relationship.

There are various steps you can take when setting boundaries with a narcissist. These include the following:

Drawing the Line

The first step in creating boundaries with a narcissist is knowing your limit. This limit encompasses the various behaviors and actions that you are willing to take from your narcissistic counterpart. Everyone has things they can tolerate, and this will differ from one person to another.

Although it is an unhealthy tolerance, some individuals tolerate a cheating partner as long as they don't resort to physical abuse. In your case, you may draw the line the moment the narcissist starts hurling insults. Once they do so, make up your mind to end the conversation abruptly.

Be assertive in doing so. This can be during a discussion with the narcissist. If there is an insult from the narcissist, you make a direct comment such as "The next time you make an insulting comment will be the end of this discussion." Once the narcissist resorts to insults, you leave without providing an opportunity for the narcissist to convince you.

When drawing the line, it is essential that you act swiftly. If you take time in leaving the conversation, you may end up getting more insults from the narcissist. This can also expose you to the gaslighting tactic of the narcissist.

The reason for drawing the line is because you know how difficult it is to change a narcissist. So instead, you can change the way you respond to the actions of the narcissist. This can prevent you from taking their actions personally and getting frustrated in the process.

By drawing the line, you prevent them from influencing you with their toxic traits by throwing them out early. Drawing the line is also a way of telling yourself that you deserve better. This is crucial in maintaining excellent self-esteem.

One of the actions you need to learn to stop using these boundaries is apologizing to the narcissist. As an object of their narcissistic supply, an apology is your way of giving in to them. The message you are passing across is that you are an insecure individual who relies on their perfection.

By identifying what you can tolerate, you can prevent any situation in which the narcissist will gaslight you into blaming yourself. Knowing what you deserve means that you don't expose yourself to any form of ridicule that will eat away at your self-esteem.

All these are achievable as soon as you decide to draw the line.

Defining Your Boundaries

When setting your boundaries with a narcissist, you must note that things won't always go as planned. There is often a need to readjust these boundaries if they don't meet your expectations. This implies that the process of defining boundaries is continuous throughout your time with a narcissist.

During this process, you should also include consequences. These consequences take effect once the narcissist crosses your boundary. From your interaction with a narcissist, you will understand that they are most likely going to ignore the boundaries you set at one point or the other.

Communication is key to the successful implementation of your boundaries. Therefore, it is crucial you communicate with the narcissist. Let them know the consequences of ignoring these boundaries.

The goal is to communicate the consequences, and you shouldn't explain to the narcissist why you are taking these steps. It is for your protection and peace of mind. If you communicate these consequences once, then that is enough to put it into effect.

Narcissists don't back down easily. This is why you must act as soon as they overstep. Failure to take action speaks to the narcissist. They interpret this as you being weak, and therefore, they will still act as before knowing that you are all talk.

When you define your boundaries, you can expect the narcissist to be more brutal in their attacks. Knowing the action the narcissist is likely going to take can help in choosing the right boundaries to set.

Make Use of an If/When List

When defining your boundaries, there is often a need to set boundaries on what you talk about with the narcissist. A narcissist can find ways to put you down based on your relationship or work. This means you want to deflect any question that may spark a conversation revolving around any of these topics.

To do this, having an if/when list can help. The "if/when" list is a list of the responses you will give to the narcissist when they ask any of these questions. The answers can help you change the topic of the conversation to something more attractive to the narcissist.

If you know that the narcissist likes to criticize your job, then there must be a response on your list for any time they ask about work. A trick to getting them to lose interest is by offering an answer that makes them focus on themselves. You should know how much narcissists enjoy being the center of attention in a conversation.

Make your list at a time when you are not under any form of pressure so that you can replay all the possible scenarios in your head. A simple response on your list can be:

- If he/she asks about my work, then I will say, "Wonderful. How did you save up so much money with ease?"

This reply focuses on the narcissists' ability to handle money. It will often result in them boasting about their skills, but it helps to prevent them from putting you down. Most times, it is best to avoid a confrontation with a narcissist.

Being prepared is your best weapon to get out of most of the tactics the narcissist tries to use.

Stop Stroking the Narcissists' Ego

You may not be making comments to flatter the narcissist, but it is possible you are currently stroking their ego with your actions. This may be in the way you act or the amount of attention you give the narcissist.

To do this, the first step is to be true to yourself. Stop acting the way the narcissist wants you to act. The way they want you to act is often a persona they develop to make them feel better about who they are while putting you down.

You can decide to be a strong and confident person around the narcissist rather than someone who is overwhelmed. You can also act in a manner that ensures that you get the respect you deserve from the narcissist.

Another way to stop stroking the ego of the narcissist is to stop giving them all the attention in every situation. To get the attention they desire, a narcissist will require you to give priority to their beliefs, needs, and what they say at any time. This means you spend all your time caring for the narcissist with less time for yourself.

To ensure you are not giving your undivided attention to the needs of the narcissist, you must remain mentally aware. This involves checking from time to time that thoughts, needs, and feelings you have during an interaction with a narcissist comes from within.

Using the Gray Rock Method to Put up a Boundary

The narcissist enjoys putting people down, and they have tactics that they use in achieving their goal. To avoid falling for these tactics, there is a need to set a boundary on how you respond when they try using these tactics on you. One effective method to put up this boundary is through the gray rock method.

The Four Types of Narcissism

The gray rock method is a technique that enables you to control your responses to the provocative actions of the narcissist either through gaslighting or triangulation. The reactions that the narcissist looks for include despair, anger, self-doubt, or confusion. The gray rock method involves giving no response to these provocative actions.

If you want to understand this better, liken the actions of the narcissist to a kid throwing tantrums. These tantrums often get you to react in a specific way in which they get what they want. Once they know they can get what they want through this action, they will keep repeating it.

On the other hand, if they have a temper tantrum and you don't show any reaction, they will calm down and choose to stop doing it after a while. The same applies to a narcissist. The narcissist is usually driven by the fact that they can get you to react to their provocations.

When they see you have no reaction to these provocations, they start doing it less often. It isn't easy to implement the gray rock method effectively since there are times when you are surely going to react. Nonetheless, it is a useful tool in creating boundaries.

Limit the Amount of Information you Feed the Narcissist

Narcissists need information from you to simplify their task of getting you to feel down. This information is what they use in criticizing you. For this reason, you must not give out too much information to the narcissist.

It can be your narcissistic parent or partner. Don't let them know every detail of your daily life. This is a boundary that will work in limiting the extent of the narcissistic abuse you receive.

Stick to it!

Setting your boundaries in your head often makes it difficult to keep track and implement it effectively in the early stages. A better option is to create physical copies of these boundaries in writing to ensure that you remember every boundary you have set in your relationship with a narcissist.

Another benefit of the physical copy is the possibility of pasting it in a location where it is visible to the narcissist. This way, you are sure they won't have the opportunity to deny the fact that you communicated the boundaries (although this won't stop them from engaging in denial).

During the period when you paste a physical copy of the boundaries, you must take time to read them every day. This is to ensure that you commit them to memory. This will make it easier for you to take swift action against the narcissist.

Earlier, I mentioned the need to leave a conversation without giving an explanation to the narcissist. This is to prevent them from making any argument that may seem convincing to you. If you feel the need to explain, then you can do so in writing.

This is when you are alone without any pressure from the narcissist. At this moment, any thought that comes to you is yours and a true reflection of how you feel. There is no form of confusion so you can get your message across to the narcissist.

To make it easier to stick to your boundaries, be sure they are things that you can implement. There is nothing worse than giving the impression that you are bluffing to the narcissist. This will prompt a more aggressive reaction from the narcissist.

One of the superweapons that you have at your disposal when dealing with a narcissist is sticking to the boundaries you set. This tells the narcissist that they can't get away with walking over you.

Try to Understand the Narcissist

Understanding the narcissist isn't the same as accepting everything the narcissist does. It is simply realizing that the narcissist is an empty and inferior individual beneath their masks. When you understand this, you know that they have limitations as humans.

Although this empathy is what narcissists use in turning an individual into a puppet, it can also help you in developing a thick-skin against most of their actions. This can prevent you from taking the actions of a narcissist personally. Regardless of how much compassion you try to show, there are limits to what you can and what you should take from the narcissist.

If you are slowly getting to this limit despite your best efforts, then there is a last resort.

Leave if You Have To

There is always the option of leaving a narcissist. Sometimes, leaving the narcissist can mean ending a conversation before it gets out of hand. This is one of the simplest ways to avoid confrontation with a narcissist.

To leave a conversation with ease, there are various tricks to pull this off. You can predetermine how much time you want to spend in a conversation with the narcissist. Once you decide on the duration, you can set your phone alarm to go off as soon as the time is up. Pretend it is a call you must take and use the opportunity to leave.

You want to leave before the narcissist gets the opportunity to become abusive or unpleasant toward you. This is one of the basics of a great boundary. The other form of leaving involves packing your bags and saying goodbye to the narcissist.

This is the best option when you find out that you can't cope with the narcissist even with excellent boundaries. This applies when the narcissist continues to disregard your boundaries despite the consequences you put in place. In a relationship, you have the right to be treated with respect. If you can't get this respect, then you know you are better off without the relationship.

Go no contact with the narcissist. The no contact method will give you more time for yourself to get back on your feet and move forward after a narcissistic relationship.

There is a problem you need to prepare for when you take this route. This is the hoovering tactic of the narcissist. They don't like it when their target decides to walk away. They want to be the one to let go of you. Hoovering is a method to get you back into the relationship.

Knowing what it is, it is vital you don't give in to the tactics of the narcissist. This is the backlash you can expect from the narcissist when you start to see them for who they are.

Creating boundaries that are effective in dealing with your narcissistic partner will take time and isn't going to be easy to achieve. Starting early is crucial in developing yourself in the art of setting healthy boundaries that can protect you from narcissistic abuse.

Boundaries don't always go down well with a narcissist. So, you should prepare yourself for an unexpected reaction from the narcissist—often a narcissistic rage. You may consider dropping the idea of creating boundaries if it will result in narcissistic rage. Don't do it.

If you decide to overlook the need to set boundaries, you are going to come out of the relationship with low self-esteem, demeaned, and confused. With the boundaries in place, you can leave with your self-esteem intact and find it easier to move on after the relationship.

Conclusion

The narcissist in your life doesn't have to destroy everything that you hold dear. You can have a narcissist in your life and still live a happy life. Learning about the narcissist will make you better at dealing with them.

This is also necessary if you want to heal from the narcissistic abuse you have been going through. There are numerous topics to help you understand the narcissist that has been covered in this book.

There was a look at the narcissistic personality disorder and the relationship with parenting styles in childhood. Although it is not always the fault of the parents, indulgent and neglectful parenting are some of the causes of narcissistic personality disorder.

An indulgent parent is one who promotes the actions of entitlement in their child while also providing an excess of possessions and privileges to the child. You will even notice a lack of discipline in the way they handle the child when they do wrong. Another parenting style that promotes narcissism is neglectful parenting.

Parents have to work to feed their kids. When this work takes all your time, there is no time left to spend with the family.

This is one of the reasons why some parents appear neglectful. In others, they want nothing to do with the child. This is common in some parents that undergo the same treatment in their childhood.

Another important topic that you must have gone through is the narcissistic supply in narcissists. This is the fuel of the narcissistic personality. Knowing this, how do they get this fuel?

There was a discussion on the various actions that narcissists employ like getting a source and adding a trigger to get the fuel. Besides, you should already have an idea of the little world of the narcissist and how it differs from the world you see.

To ensure you are not unaware of what is happening to you, I shifted your focus to the common tactics that the narcissist uses if it is time to bring you down. These tactics can be destructive and have a lasting impression on the victims. They include the gaslighting, triangulation, and smear campaigns.

Another common tactic is the idealization, devaluation, and discard tactic of the narcissist, which is in place throughout your relationship with a narcissist. This tactic occurs in the form of a cycle, and there is no limit to the number of cycles you may experience before the end of the abuse.

The second part of this book was an introduction to the various types of narcissists you can meet. These include the grandiose, communal, covert, and malignant narcissist. Each narcissist differs from the others, but this doesn't mean that they are not all equally dangerous.

The most troublesome of them all, in my opinion, is the covert narcissist because they are discreet in their narcissistic action. You might have all the information on the overt behaviors of a narcissist while still under the influence of the covert narcissist without knowing. That is how troublesome they can get. They do not exhibit most of the traits that make it easy to spot a narcissist.

The next part of this book is a look at the recovery tactics to assist you in overcoming the abuse from the narcissist. The first set of tactics involve understanding the obstacles you need to overcome.

Various obstacles make it difficult to recover from narcissistic abuse. Some of these obstacles are the starvation of love, psychological trap, low self-esteem, low shame tolerance, the lack of shame, lack of boundaries, fear, and guilt. These obstacles are like chains that are holding you back.

Breaking free from these chains is essential if you are to recover from the abuse. Inability to break free means that even after escaping the narcissistic relationship, you will still find yourself reliving the trauma from the abuse.

The second set of tactics involve creating a support structure. Getting over narcissistic abuse is complicated and isn't something that you should go through on your own. Thankfully, you can create support structures to assist you in the process. You can start by involving your friends and family as allies.

This step is possible if the narcissist hasn't turned them against you. There will surely be a group of people that will remain loyal to you regardless of the actions of the narcissist. You can also go on to find support groups that can assist.

Most of us are quite familiar with support groups due to their influence in helping others get over addictions and other challenges. There are specific support groups dedicated to victims of narcissistic abuse. The main benefit of these groups is the possibility of meeting people that understand what you are going through and learning from those that have overcome the abuse.

Learning to restore your self-esteem is also crucial in recovery. It is only through this action that you can fully appreciate yourself. When dealing with a narcissist, there are traps that they set to keep you engaged and acting as their supply.

The emotional investment trap, conversation trap, and humor trap are all things you should avoid. Your final tactic towards recovery is creating boundaries.

Ironclad boundaries will limit the effect of narcissistic abuse. It can also prevent the abuse entirely. It is a tactic that appears simple but yields excellent results in actions toward recovery.

This book promised to help you understand narcissists, deal with them, and recover from their abuse. To deliver on this promise, I broke down this book into three parts. The first and second parts of this book focus on helping you understand the narcissist. Who are they? How do they act? Why are they the way they are?

The content on the third part covers topics that help you in dealing with narcissists and recovering from their abuse. In its entirety, this book is a breakdown of everything you can expect from a narcissistic relationship and dealing with those things.

The Four Types of Narcissism

There are so many things you can take away from this book, but there is one thing I keep telling my readers to pick. While you may not find it written explicitly in the book, what I want you to take away is the fact that running away from the narcissist isn't always your best option.

Dealing with the narcissist should be your best solution. Going no contact with the narcissist should be an option you choose as a last resort. There is a simple reason why I tell this to my readers.

Ask yourself a question, what happens if you come across another narcissist tomorrow? Are you going to keep running away from relationships? What if you never find the perfect partner?

There are times when there is no sign that the relationship with the narcissist will ever get better. There are other times when you can improve the relationship. This is what you must keep in mind before making your final decision.

References

Grohol, J. (2019). The Big Five Personality Traits. Retrieved 20 September 2019, from https://psychcentral.com/lib/the-big-five-personality-traits/

Lancer, D. (2019). 7 Things to Know about Irrational Guilt - dummies. Retrieved 21 September 2019, from https://www.dummies.com/health/mental-health/codependency/7-things-to-know-about-irrational-guilt/

Legg, T. (2018). Narcissistic personality disorder: Traits, diagnosis, and treatment. Retrieved 20 September 2019, from https://www.medicalnewstoday.com/articles/9741.php

Simon, G. (2016). Grandiose Narcissists - Dr. George Simon. Retrieved 20 September 2019, from https://www.drgeorgesimon.com/grandiose-narcissists/

Raypole, C., & Leng, T. (2019). Malignant Narcissism: What It Actually Means. Retrieved 11 September 2019, from https://www.healthline.com/health/malignant-narcissism

Seltzer, L. (2015). This Is What Really Makes Narcissists Tick. Retrieved 21 September 2019, from https://www.psychologytoday.com/us/blog/evolution-the-self/201507/is-what-really-makes-narcissists-tick

Streep, P. (2016). The Communal Narcissist: Another Wolf Wearing a Sheep Outfit. Retrieved 20 September 2019, from https://www.psychologytoday.com/us/blog/tech-support/201605/the-communal-narcissist-another-wolf-wearing-sheep-outfit

Thompson, D. (2015). Overindulgent Parents May Breed Narcissistic Children. Retrieved 20 September 2019, from https://consumer.healthday.com/mental-health-information-25/behavior-health-news-56/overindulgent-parents-may-breed-narcissistic-children-697258.html

Made in the USA
Columbia, SC
21 May 2023